"I've had the good fortun recognizable names in the political arenas; and to say our best guests would be an understatement. His ability to connect, inspire and impact viewers through the use of entertainment is unlike anything I've seen before; and to now have a book that delivers powerful 'common sense' messages to help people succeed is fantastic! Now you have Gregg Amerman at your fingertips...take advantage of it!"

> *– Conn Jackson*
> *Television and Radio Personality*

"I truly believe you change your life when you change your thinking, and this book will give you countless opportunities to change your thinking and your life! Gregg Amerman does it again!"

> *– Les Brown*
> *World Renowned Speaker and Best Selling Author*

"As a CEO of my own business, managing a family with two young children and being the wife of Mario Cristobal, head football coach at the University of Oregon, I'm always looking for an edge. The success principles within this book are effective to apply in every area of our lives. This book is the perfect guide to becoming the best you can be."

> *– Jessica Cristobal*
> *Founder and CEO, Leading Ladies League, Inc.*

"In his own unique style and approach to life, Gregg Amerman, in this enjoyable and easy to read book, gives us a common sense approach with humor and wit on how to reach our individual goals and aspirations. It's a must read!"

> *– Ramie A. Tritt, MD*
> *Physician, Entrepreneur of the Year*

"I've had some of the best coaches in baseball history and Gregg Amerman is one of the best coaches for personal success. By reading this book, you will know the key elements for achieving results and what it takes to be a champion! Read it many times!"

– Dave Parker
Nineteen-Year MLB Career, MVP, World Series Champion

"Gregg Amerman is one of the most talented writers you'll ever read because it's written the way he speaks. You literally feel like he's talking directly to you and that's why it's so impactful. This book is easy to read and understand and very entertaining. You'll be nodding your head *yes* throughout. We laughed and reflected, but mostly we said, 'Everyone has to read this book!'"

– Joe and JaDee Locke
Co-Founder, Entrepreneurs International

"Gregg is a gifted and talented speaker and author. This book is just like Gregg on stage—candid, truthful, straightforward, real, and, of course, humorous. This book has the entire basis for wealth and success, all you have to do is live it. The rest is history!"

– James Smith
Wealth Strategist and Real Estate Mogul

Things That Make You Go . . .
Hmmm

Things That
Make You Go . . .
Hmmm

Gregg Amerman

**_BOOK_LOGIX®**

Alpharetta, GA

ISBN: 978-1-61005-575-8

Library of Congress Control Number: 2015900948

10 9 8 7 6 5 4 3 2   0 3 2 0 1 9

Printed in the United States of America

∞This paper meets the requirements of ANSI/NISO Z39.48-1992 (Permanence of Paper)

This book has two very significant dedications:

The first is to my dad who I miss and think about quite often. He passed away at the young age of fifty-five while I was only twenty-one years old and still in college. My dad was a great man who gave me many opportunities throughout my younger years and was a tremendous positive influence in my life. He ultimately played a major role in shaping me into the man I am today. While I know my dad never got to physically see me graduate from college, begin my entrepreneurial career, or witness my marriage and the birth of my children or see me speak from the biggest of stages and make a huge difference in many people's lives, I know my dad saw it all in sprit. I truly believe he is extremely proud of all of my accomplishments, both personally and professionally. I love you dad . . . this book is for you!

The second dedication is to all the individuals who have the yearning desire to achieve greatness in their life and who have the eagerness to think, learn, grow, and change like I did. It's not just good enough to want it, you have to go out and get it, and that is whom this book is for. It feels great to know this book is in the right hands.

Contents

Acknowledgments

If someone were to ask me what was the hardest part of authoring this book, believe it or not, it would be this section. How do I express gratitude to so many people that deserve a "thank you" for the accomplishments I've been able to enjoy in my life? I have always believed that there is no such thing as a self-made success because success always requires the help of other people. While it is my intent to acknowledge the many friends, family members, team members, colleagues, and positive influences along my journey, I also want to apologize in advance if I unintentionally overlooked someone deserving of being recognized.

I would like to start with the one person who has played the most critical role in my life and has supported me at the lowest of lows and the highest of highs! My mom, Sandy Amerman, who, without question, did a great job of raising me and providing for me, but even more importantly, believed in me when no one else did. At the age of twenty-five, when I began my first entrepreneurial endeavor, my mom really got behind me. She invested in me financially when she was in no position to do so. My mom opened up her home and her heart and was my number one fan, enthusiast, and partner. Honestly, regardless of how I've been able to provide for my mom in recent years, I will never be able to repay or thank my mom for all she has done for me.

Secondly, I want to thank my best friend and wife, Frenita. Frenita is an amazing woman in her own right but, in my eyes, her most meaningful trait is her loyalty. Talk about unconditional love—which certainly defines my wife— Frenita takes her commitment seriously and certainly understands the meaning of "through richer or poorer" and "thick or thin". Frenita has always been there. I now know what love is and, while Frenita may not be perfect, because none of us are, Frenita is perfect for me! Thanks for believing in me and allowing me to be who I am and, most importantly, loving who I am not what I am.

I have a special appreciation and love for my three wonderful children, Kellen, Kaleigh and Kolten, who've often times missed their dad at some of their school programs, sporting events, or other special activities as I was on the road conducting training programs or just working really long hours. So much of my commitment is dedicated to my kids having more and getting a chance to be more, and I am very thankful that my children understand what I'm doing and love me more because of it. I have a love for what I do and a love for why I do it—my family!

I am also blessed to have an extraordinary family with great in-laws! Much of what I've been able to do is because of Frenita's parents, Fred and Juanita Henderson. Whatever we've needed and whenever we've needed them, they have been there. They always say yes. Thanks for everything!

Other family members I want to acknowledge for being there throughout my career and life are Jeff and Paula Amerman, Larry and Elaine Amerman, Sonja Chunn, Daniel Amerman, and Matthew Amerman.

Thanks to Van and Martha Halbreich, I call them my second parents. They have taken a genuine interest in my success and me for many years. They have been great supporters, fans, and encouragers. You are great people with some of the biggest hearts of any people I have ever met. I love you guys.

A special thanks to Dr. Ramie Tritt, a mentor, a business partner, a motivator, and a friend; a man who helped get this book to publishing; but mostly a man who is a great role model on how to have integrity, on conducting business the right way, on being generous and giving, and, especially, on being a family man. Thank you for epitomizing what everyone should strive to achieve.

While there are many people throughout my career who have been a part of my journey, one individual stands out as the best teammate and most reliable partner I could possibly have. This true friend of 30 years is not only extremely talented, but one of the most humble and loyal people I could be associated with. Thank you Joe Locke for being back-to-back with me on an amazing ride to the top.

To the individuals behind the scenes who not only make up the best team I could possibly be a part of but also who happen to be some of my longest standing friends who have battled with me through many endeavors. Neil Waite, Price Wilkes, Mark "Soda" Soderquist, Kelly Wilson, Brian Hansen, Kevin Miller, Kevin Walker, Stephanie Roberts, Shawna Stevenson and many more. None of this is possible without you.

To a great group of battle-tested comrades. I've known these six loyal, dedicated individuals anywhere from five to twenty years; and I've never met a group that understands and exhibits the true essence of "team" any more than they do. The relationships that have evolved and the growth I've seen in each and every one of these people as trainers, as entrepreneurs, and as human beings, makes me proud to call them dear friends. Thank you Jill Halbreich, Mike Miller, Orlando McKenzie, Darrel Gentry, Warren Bauerfeld and Michael Johnson for your core strength and core values.

Then there are many folks from both the past and the present who have been a part of my life and my success. Some maybe in a small way and some in a very significant way. I appreciate you JaDee Locke, Romeo and Lisa House, Ron and Carla Lewis, Cynthia Davis, Mario and Jessica Cristobal, Lawrence Turner, Lorna Miller, Joe Esser, Tim Mitchell, Tony Swiantek, Bryan Moore, Chris Calloway, Conn Jackson, Jeffrey Kess, Stephen Fuller, Dave Parker,

Deborah Battle, Johnny Trotter, Lorne Tritt, Patrick Lane, Deon Robinson, Elzy Tubbs, Kimanne Parr, George Andersen, Terrance and Ekeena Smalls, Mark Bustamonte, Ricky Frank, Wayne Garland, Jermaine Jackson, Toney Freeman, Denise Russo, Carl Merriweather, Paul Miles, Chuck Pereira, Scott and Diane McKnight, James Smith, Jonathan Ginsberg, Kari Michaelsen, Larry Cianelli, Lilly Ortiz, Lisa Singletary, Elizabeth Link, Terri Amador, Angela Talbert, Joel Athy, Lucretia Daniel, Marc Western, Ron Lewis, Sue Bauerfeld, Michelle Cook, Pat Scordio, Patty Luna, Pete Hajjar, Raul and Theresa Padilla, Rick Newby, Robert Mehler, Rod Warren, Ron Morehead, Russell Levine, Steve Ulp, Phil Rodriguez, Tara Haskoor, Theo Ratliff, Byron Hall, Tracy Green, Yvette Reid, Melissa Fowler, Gene Berman, Rick Ruperto, John Rubischko, Alesa Flowers, Carlos Binns, Harrison Gilmer, Carnell Newsome, Chad Lance, Joe O'Reilly, Dan Marcacci, Frank Doherty, Cory Blackwell, Dick Whiting, Janis Greenfield, Joel Hefley, Keith Fraley, and Les Brown. All of you, thanks for being a part of my success and my life!

Wow! I am so humbled by all the wonderful people I have in my life that have not only contributed to my achievements but, more importantly, who are getting to share in it as well. While many great things have happened over the years, the best part is there's much more to look forward to! Thanks again to everyone!

"SHORTCUTS: How challenging would the game of golf be if there was a tube from the tee box to the hole, and every time you hit a ball it was a hole-in-one? It wouldn't be, and no one would want to play! Same in life and business; true success comes from your ability to develop your mindset and skillset as well as your ability to overcome all the obstacles and challenges along the way, taking one shot at a time! No Shortcuts!**"

Preface

Things That Make You Go Hmmm . . .

Growing up, I was definitely a big-time dreamer. I was going to be a professional basketball player, so of course there was zero doubt I would have a massive house with a huge pool, a game room, and an indoor and outdoor basketball court. I would own an array of exotic sports cars and a yacht and I would travel the world and have the freedom to spend time with my friends and family. I'm sure you can relate; you probably had similar dreams (except for maybe the basketball player part) and maybe even bigger ones. Well, a few things happened between then and the time I began living in the "the real world."

I grew up in Queens, New York. The house I lived in was what's called a brick row house, which means it was literally attached to the one next door. You could basically shake hands with your neighbor without walking out the front door. There were three bedrooms and one full bathroom with a shower, shared with my parents and two older brothers. I always had to share a room with my brothers until they went to college. Overall, the close quarters didn't really bother me because I didn't know any better. The funniest part was our backyard, which was made of cement, so it wasn't really a backyard—it was a back alley. Our front yard was the street but that was okay because it served as our football and baseball field. When we played football, the parked cars were our end zones, and for baseball, our bases were manhole covers and streetlights. It's amazing how creative and resourceful you can be when you want to do something badly enough—and playing sports was something most of the kids on our block loved to do, plus it was one of the only things *available* to do. Eventually, I became most passionate about basketball, and even though I played pretty much every day and talked about making it to the NBA, that dream never came to fruition. (Today, I know why, and I will soon share with you the great lessons I learned; if I knew then what I know now, who knows, maybe I wouldn't have written this book because I would have played in the NBA.)

My dad was something of an entrepreneur; he had his own accounting practice and tried several other business ventures through the years. His accounting business did okay, and we were happy, so I guess you would say we were pretty much the average American family. That is, until our normal life came to a halt when my dad unexpectedly died at the age of fifty-five. I was twenty-one at the time, and, as anyone who has suddenly lost a loved one can understand, it was devastating. When the shock and grieving was over, the harsh reality of life set in: my dad was gone and so were the business and the income that had been our support. My mom—who had always helped my dad with his business but primarily took care of the household and raising three boys—found herself looking for a job. It was a sobering experience to see my family in financial distress. Watching all of what the future was supposed to be for my parents, who talked about the golden years and the life they were going to have, completely vanish was my first wake-up call—and an extremely valuable lesson.

While my first desire was to help my mom, I also wanted to make sure I avoided a similar situation down the road. My dad had achieved admirable success by building something for himself. He just didn't follow one important key principle: incorporating the efforts of other people. Had he done that, his business and its income would have lived on long after him. Upon recognizing this, I realized that the responsibility of how my life would evolve rested squarely on my shoulders.

I was never what you would call a dedicated student. I was the kid who sat as far back in the class as I could and daydreamed the majority of the time. School just wasn't fun for me, so often while the teacher rambled on about whatever the lesson was for that day, I was thinking about other things I wanted to do. I was a C student at best, and although today I would probably be labeled as ADHD, back then I was just considered a poor student and a class clown. Compounding that was that my oldest brother was an academic genius who got straight As and was the ideal student so, as you might imagine, I heard quite a bit of, "Why can't you be more like your brother?" It was at that point I perfected how to roll my eyes.

I finally got through high school, but with my grades being so low, I had to attend Queensborough Community College because no four-year school would accept me. You might think maybe I was ready to buckle down and take education more seriously. Nope. I continued to daydream and find every reason not to go to class or to work very hard on my education. And I was so off track that during one semester I literally dropped every class just to avoid failing them all. Eventually, after finishing two and a half years at a two-year school without receiving a degree (that's probably some kind of accomplishment in itself, not a good one, but an accomplishment), I transferred to Springfield College in Massachusetts. I couldn't believe I got in but I think the reason I was accepted was because my interviewer, John Wilson from admissions, liked me and made some things happen to get me in. I loved being there, and it was probably one of the best social experiences of my life but one thing hadn't changed: my seriousness about attending class and focusing on the subject matter. You see, as a dreamer, I never thought that the courses I took were going to be applicable in my world. I was in school because I thought I had to be, because everyone told me that was what I needed to do to be successful, not because I saw purpose in being there or because I had a passion for this so-called valuable education. In the end, after a total of six and a half years, I did emerge a college graduate—though my GPA of 1.9 probably didn't do any good for the college's academic average. But you know what? I felt good about being able to say I was a college graduate, and the cool thing is, as my degree is displayed on my office wall, it looks every bit as good as everyone else's because they don't print your GPA on your diploma. How about that?

Of course, getting through school was a major financial challenge because, with my dad being gone, I really had to support myself. That meant I had to spend my summers working to save up some money for the school year. I was lucky though because my friend's uncle was a bigwig at Canada Dry and ran one of the bottling plants, we were hired to work on the assembly line. I couldn't believe it— they paid us $18 an hour and $27 an hour for overtime! I had no idea at the time that this would be the highest paying "real job" I would ever have.

This job also gave me an eye-opening perspective of how millions of people spend their days and lives. I had numerous jobs on the assembly line but none more tedious and brain numbing than working on a machine called the rinser (basically a giant dishwasher for bottles). Just imagine watching conveyor belts carrying thousands of empty one-liter plastic bottles to be washed prior to them getting filled with soda. My job was to make sure the bottles stayed standing up in order to go through the machine properly. If a bottle or multiple bottles fell down, I had to pick them up quickly to avoid having the bottles jam up in the machine. I did this for eight to twelve hours a day. Of course, as with anything, it was interesting and cool at first but boy it didn't take long for that novelty to wear off. We weren't even allowed to talk to anyone, listen to music, read, nothing. We just repeated the same motions over and over again, hour after hour, as the loud machines rang in my ears. Even earplugs couldn't drown out the nonstop noise.

It was on that assembly line that I began to see how we could just exist and basically start the process of dying while just standing in place. The work required no thought, and I therefore searched for any form of distraction. My imagination ran wild, and I even began to think about things you shouldn't think about (like orchestrating a bank robbery or how to win the lottery). I was going crazy! And when I wasn't daydreaming, I thought about all the other people around me who had been working there for decades. I knew what kinds of thoughts I was having, so I couldn't fathom what was going on in their heads. I believed some of them had just stopped thinking altogether because this was their final destination; this assembly line was all there was for the rest of their working lives. That was a scary thought for a young college kid like me.

After graduating, I returned to Canada Dry to save up some money and start repaying my school loans, but I didn't last very long. I couldn't take it anymore. Just like in my school years, I was outspoken and I questioned the way things were done and that rallied some of the other workers to do the same. Well, the bosses didn't like that. So when I quit, they made me sign a letter stating that I was resigning from the union and that I would never come back. It was the easiest agreement I've ever had to sign!

I was finally ready to use my degree in psychology, and after a few short stints working as a counselor with teenagers, I made the move into what would be my last structured job: a foster care social worker in the heart of New York. Every day, I saw the struggles of distressed families and things nobody—especially kids—should see: drug abuse, violence, poverty, and much more. I couldn't have imagined having to live like this. Many times, I just found myself shaking my head in disbelief. I wanted so badly to help these families and children but it was a continuous struggle dealing with bureaucratic red tape, confusing rules, laws, and regulations, and the fact that I could barely survive on what I was being paid. I certainly understood that social work wasn't a high-paying profession but I never could reconcile the fact that I made twice as much money sitting on my backside watching bottles on a conveyor belt.

It was kind of a bizarre twist because what started out as a goal of helping the less fortunate ended up with *me* becoming less fortunate in terms of my finances. I was earning $582 every two weeks, paying someone $200 a month to rent a room, and driving a Hyundai I paid less than $9,000 for—brand-new—but for which I was still three months behind in the car payments. The only reason I needed a rearview mirror was to look out for the repo man. I just knew there had to be a better way—a better way to help people on a much larger scale and a better way to earn a living in order to fulfill those expensive dreams I had as a kid.

I always believed there were three ways to make money. You could make money hurting people, and there were certainly people doing that. You could make money doing nothing for people, and there were plenty of people doing that. Or you could make money helping people. That's what I wanted to do—it was just a matter of finding out how.

As more and more time went by, I grew tired of the constant struggle to make ends meet. My frustration rose to a boil. I wanted a better way of life! A better life for my mom, a better life for myself, and ultimately, one day, a better life for as many people as I could help.

Finally, something inside me snapped. I told myself, "I'm going to change my life. I don't want to stay where I am any longer and I'm going to do something about it. I'm going to find a new way, a new path, to something better." It was that change in attitude that set in motion the forces that would change my life forever.

One day on my way to work, I bought a newspaper. At my desk, I opened it to the classifieds section. It was the first time I ever actively searched for a job—each one before I had gotten through a referral. I remembered hearing that sales was the most lucrative profession so I turned to the sales section and found an ad that read, "Wild and Crazy, make $10,000 a month." I was pretty naïve at the time so to say I was excited about that prospect was an understatement. But the best part of the whole experience unfolded when a coworker asked what I was doing. I told her, "I can't do this anymore—I've got to go." I showed her the ad and I'll never forget her response: "That's got to be a scam." Without even thinking, I replied, "Hey, I don't care. Staying here's *making* me crazy, so yeah, I'm feeling a little wild. Anything's got to be better than this."

When I look back at that exact moment, it stands out as a pivotal one for me because I could have been influenced by this doubtful coworker. I could have listened to her and allowed her skepticism and negativity to become my own and that would have cost me the opportunity of a lifetime. I could still be . . . no, I don't even want to think about it. I still look back on that situation as illustrative of two of the most powerful lessons of my life: one, be careful whom you listen to, and two, every decision you make will affect the rest of your life. Thank goodness I had such a passion for change that I listened to my inner voice (you'll be hearing about that more in a later section) and not my coworker. Who would have thought that the first ad I ever answered would also be my last?

This led me to the discovery of sales, marketing, and network marketing—a concept I had never even heard of. Any thought of owning a business was not even realistic to me. How could *I*—somebody who barely earned a degree and was scraping by to rent a room to sleep in at night—own a business? There were all these perceived obstacles in my way. You've got to have a lot of money—something I definitely didn't have. You need a lot of time because you think of having a store, which is open regular hours that you have to be available for. You couldn't possibly own a business on the side while working your day job. And finally, you had to be smart with a degree in business or years of experience, of which I had none.

Well, that's what blew me away. Because when I attended the first business presentation and I came to understand what they were offering, it changed my whole perception. This was the first time I said, "hmmm," but I didn't understand what hmmm was at that point—that came much later. I was just totally in awe of this newfound opportunity. I'll never forget it. There were ten people sitting in the same presentation as me and, after it was over, all of them got up and left. I was the only one who stayed. Watching them file out, I kept thinking, "Where are they going? Don't they see it? Don't they get it? This is the greatest thing ever!"

I couldn't believe I could start a business with virtually no money and with limited time. I could actually start out by keeping my job, and the fact that I didn't need any experience was amazing to me. It was something totally foreign to me and yet I was so excited about the possibilities.

For those of you by chance who may not be familiar with the network marketing industry, let me give you a quick understanding. It's a type of business model where a company has a product or service to offer and takes that product or service to the marketplace through independent contractors. The company pays commissions based on the personal volume of products and services you sell and on the total sales volumes of the distributors who have been recruited onto your team, which is called your organization. It's a very simple but brilliant concept and it gives the average person who never thought they could own a business that exact opportunity. Same thing for anyone looking for a simple, low overhead operation because it only requires a small initial investment to get started. It's a business that is built by sweat investment. The harder you work and the more products and services you and your team move, the more successful you become.

What I loved most was that my lack of experience wasn't a hindrance because other people already well-versed in the business were willing to teach me what they knew. The marketing structure gave them a vested interest in my success.

Although I have endured many trials, tribulations, and obstacles in my career, I can truthfully say I was fortunate in that I was immediately introduced to a system with a successful leader and mentor at the helm. This mentor took me under his wing and, believe me, I took full advantage of it. I was an eager and respectful student. Suddenly, I— someone who never made it through a class without getting swept away in daydreams—became an avid student of another kind of education—that of his own success. I was a constant participant at trainings, seminars, workshops, and boot camps. In fact, over the years, I have probably invested more than $100,000 to attend all of those programs, including traveling, hotels, and meals, and investing in all the other audio/video programs and other business tools I could get my hands on. I was on fire to become the best at my craft, to become a professional, to be the best I could be.

I saw this experience very similarly to my formal education, except this was a subject I was genuinely interested in. And I was willing to work hard to do well. Here, my grade was not measured by a letter—an A, B, or C—but by a number—a paycheck number. I might have gotten Ds in school but now I was getting checks with multiple zeros on them.

My mentor understood that, like me, most people didn't know how to build a business like this—or any business, for that matter. He understood that most people are not trained for success but more for mere mediocrity and they needed to learn how to become more than that. So he created a training system that allowed a willing and receptive student to learn the business while also seeing the value in his or her own personal growth and development. I was in a whole new world, and suddenly I was doing something that I hadn't done in a long time: THINKING. New ideas, concepts, and philosophies flooded my mind as I realized how little I really knew and understood. All this helped me to figure out why success had eluded me up to this point in my life.

So now I was ready for that success. I had a system, the tools, a great business, and infinite opportunities to grow. I was no longer stuck in a rut, going nowhere—getting more broke and more frustrated by the day. Those days were over!

Ultimately, I found a way to make more money than I ever imagined and a way to help my mom. This job was perfect for me because I had found my "dream job"—getting paid to help people. As I had always known, there really was a way to help people and make a fortune while doing it. In addition, I ended up with something much better: a reason to live my life every day. While I knew I needed to think about the future, planning, and retirement, I also began living for *right now.* I had seen that my dad never made it to the future and that changed everything about the way I lived my life. I made sure that wasn't going to happen by putting myself on a course where I could control my own success— not be controlled by focusing too much on tomorrow but focusing on the NOW.

For the next decade, I worked with three different companies. It was a wild ride and it eventually led to something much better.

The experience allowed me to develop talents I never knew I had. The business placed me in situations that were forging me into who I was supposed to really be and what I was really supposed to do. Having to do constant business presentations and trainings and having to talk to countless people, both one-on-one and in group settings, set the stage for what was soon to become my niche. I had always loved speaking and training others and I was good at it. As I got better, the idea of turning my full attention and passion to creating seminars and teaching others became a reality. Eventually, I achieved another dream—creating my own brand, my own system, utilizing my own ideas and creativity, and, ultimately, building a successful company that produced great success for people!

I began training and motivating individuals, groups, organizations, and corporations in numerous areas: leadership, sales skills, establishing relationships, effective communication, teamwork, delivering excellent customer service, having a positive attitude, and much more. I also continued my passion of training individuals in network marketing, all of who had the same fire in their eyes for greatness as I did. I shared proven methods that had worked for me.

In this book (which, by the way, represents another dream I was able to achieve), I'll share plenty with you, too—namely, strategies and philosophies that will give you an edge in life and business and relationships.

Here's my ultimate goal for everyone who reads this book: I know if it can make you laugh a little and at the same time make you think a little, then you'll wake up to all that is available to you. And believe me, it's time to wake up! It's time to stop being a walking zombie. It's time to stop just existing. In the pages that follow are proven methods that will allow you to do just that by opening up your mind, offering you new ideas on how you can apply them to become not just better, but different in everything you do, from work to friendships to family. You'll learn that, believe it or not, you weren't born to fit in—you were born to stand out!

Think about this: if you asked most people to think back five years and describe what their life would be like today, in the majority of cases, their lives would be nowhere near the vision they had. Most would be pretty much in the same place they were. Sounds all too familiar, doesn't it? But the real question is, *why?* Simple answer: The number of the year has changed but you have not. The reality is, if five years from now you expect to be somewhere else, you better start being someone else today!

So are you ready for change? As you'll soon discover, change starts with something I call hmmm. That's right: hmmm. So what are you waiting for? Turn the page and find out what hmmm is and get ready to become something new, something different, and something much better. And get ready to start living a different life—one filled with financial abundance, glowing personal fulfillment, and overwhelming success.

"FAIR: Business ain't fair! Opportunities ain't fair! Life ain't fair! Stop asking and expecting everything to be fair and start striving and living for it to be *Worth It!"*

Introduction

What is . . . Hmmm?

At this point, you may be asking yourself: "**Hmmm**? What does this Gregg Amerman guy exactly mean by *Things that Make You Go **Hmmm**?* What kind of title is that for a book? Why *should* I go **hmmm**?" Or maybe you've read the preface, and you're still looking for a reason to continue. So, let's talk a little bit about this concept of **hmmm** and why it's so important to your financial future, your personal fulfillment, and your significant success.

Think for a second what's happening when the sound "**hmmm**" comes out of your mouth. Maybe you're reading a book or watching a movie, or you've just overheard an interesting conversation where someone made an enlightening point, or you were fascinated by someone doing something you hadn't seen before. Almost immediately, your mind—and sometimes your mouth too—goes **hmmm**, doesn't it? It's almost an involuntary reaction to stop, pause, and, most importantly, consider. And these **hmmms** can be for the gain of good or for the protection from bad. **Hmmm** is like your special power if you were a superhero but, of course (as with anything), it will only work for you if you believe you have it and if you use it.

That's part of what **hmmm** is: a stopping point. It makes you stand still for a moment as you ponder a feeling, a thought, or an idea. **Hmmm** is what happens when you turn over a new way of thinking in your mind. **Hmmm** can lead to a new invention, a new beginning, a new future, a new life. **Hmmm** presents an opportunity for growth. **Hmmm** creates the chance to decline or accept, to stay where you are or to move forward in another direction. Every time you have a **hmmm** moment, you change—sometimes a little, sometimes a lot.

That change—the one that starts the instant your consciousness goes "**hmmm**"—*is what this book is about.*

So here goes the first **hmmm** concept of the book. Now, I know for some of you the protesting will begin as soon as you read it. But do yourself a favor, don't react—just hear me out. Because what you're about to experience is based solely upon proven, tried, and documented truths: *There are no new ideas.*

We can probably agree that things like personal growth, achievement, advancement, accumulation of wealth, action, and bottom-line results don't just happen via spontaneous combustion or because our Fairy Godmother points her magic wand and says, "Bibbidi-Bobbidi-Boo" (I was inspired by my daughter Kaleigh who at three years old walked around saying that, believing that would actually work). Such developments, though they might have tangible results and evidence, first begin as something intangible: *a thought.* A number of years ago, the National Science Foundation estimated that humans produce between 12,000 and 50,000 thoughts per day. These thoughts are influenced by a number of sources: family members, spouses, parents, friends, teachers, coaches, mentors, a book you read, a movie you watched, or a radio program you heard in the car. Some people—even me!—actually were provoked into a thought or two during school.

Through imagination, vision, and a whole lot of your neurons firing, these thoughts might transform into an idea and that idea may become an endless source of success. All great inventions, businesses, and everything else that has a physical form—from the pet rock, to the display in a store window, to the sandwich you had for lunch, to the light bulb—began as a thought. So, this is where the **hmmm** comes in: there are no new ideas—they all develop from existing thoughts and other ideas. They all begin as a seed somewhere else—from a person, a circumstance, or an event. Think about the electric light—wasn't it a process? It's not like Thomas Edison was a caveman and the first form of light was a light bulb. There was fire, candles, and oil-burning lamps; in other words, while Thomas Edison was certainly a genius, his true genius came from listening to his **hmmm!** He had a seed to work with, a previous inspiration, and the ability to advance the evolution of something that had already existed. But the key is, he moved to action—he took the thought in his head and turned it into a life-changing apparatus. You have seeds and inspirations to work with; the question is, will you move to action as he did?

When we consider the **hmmm** about the origin of ideas, it's also helpful to look at what happens to those ideas. How many clever creations have you developed in your head that now appear on the shelves of stores making someone else millions of dollars? How many times have you heard about a new service, product, or business and smacked your forehead and berated yourself: "I already thought of that!" We are literally swimming in a sea of information that can lead to infinite ideas. They are always there waiting for someone—maybe you—to claim them.

Now that we understand that big ideas first start with a thought, we must realize that statistically the odds of acting on those ideas are stacked against us. Why? Because—and don't take this personally!—most of us haven't productively and actively thought in years. Instead, what's going on in the heads of most people you see on the street, at the office, on the highway drudging through rush-hour traffic, or even in your own home is stagnation—people just going through the motions. Sure, they're generating thoughts but those thoughts are often on a virtual loop that constantly repeat like the video at the dentist's office. Many of us who have corporate jobs we are unhappy with can identify: wake up, shower, brush teeth, get dressed, grab breakfast on the run, go to work, take a break, more work, grab lunch, go back to work, drive home, flip on the tube, eat dinner, collapse into bed. This happens day after day, week after week, year after year. Pretty soon, you look at the calendar and thirty years have passed by and your dreams are still just that—dreams.

To put it another way: Those people who do realize their dreams—and, by that standard, must be considered successful—think very differently than those who are just going through the motions. In his book *Rich Dad, Poor Dad*, author Robert Kiyosaki writes, "One dad had a habit of saying, 'I can't afford it.' The other dad forbade those words to be used. He insisted I say, 'How can I afford it?' One is a statement and the other a question. One lets you off the hook and the other forces you to think." (And that's a **hmmm** concept if I've ever heard one.)

In Napoleon Hill's book *Think and Grow Rich* (the first book I read as I began my new way of thinking and one of the best-selling books of all time), Hill asserts that "Thoughts are things" and "What the mind of man can conceive and believe, it can achieve." The title of this classic of success literature says it all. He said that those dedicated to an idea could achieve success: "There is one quality which one must possess to win, and that is definiteness of purpose, the knowledge of what one wants, and a burning desire to possess it." According to Hill, 98 percent of people have no firm beliefs, putting true success firmly out of reach for them.

Unfortunately, I tend to agree with Hill (though I would hope the number is not as high as 98 percent). So many people have been programmed to follow rather than lead. Or, they're too busy sulking or stressing over how tough life is or how badly they've been burned in a business deal or a romantic relationship instead of focusing on what they can accomplish. So their thoughts just swirl around their minds like falling leaves on a breezy fall afternoon without the possibility of an idea sticking and taking hold.

Oh, but there are others—are you one of them?—who stop and grasp onto a thought like a child clings to a dream. And then everything changes. You've stopped dead in your tracks and you find yourself saying, "**Hmmm.**"

On a much bigger scale, **hmmm** is about evolution. Charles Darwin—who created the theory of evolution—believed that species develop through helpful mutations. Over time, species develop traits that are passed down from generation to generation, constantly improving and adapting to enable the species to survive and flourish. Long, sharp teeth made wildcats better hunters. Feathers allowed a bird to soar above danger. Opposable thumbs allowed our human ancestors to grasp tools and perform tasks. These traits, once acquired, allowed some species to grow and thrive while those without them ceased to exist.

Even today, when we don't evolve, we threaten ourselves with a type of extinction. Maybe we're still breathing but, in some ways, we're already dead. Many people reach the end of their lives and think of what they *didn't* accomplish, goals they didn't reach, rather than what they did. If given the chance, they'd want to do things differently—a truly regretful thought. So how do we go about avoiding that moment in time when it seems too late?

Start by building a life that embraces **hmmm**. Start right here with this book. You'll begin to appreciate the power of **hmmm**. You'll start thinking new thoughts, embracing new ideas, and processing new philosophies. Then everything will begin to change, whether success for you means financial wealth, achieving a sense of spirituality, possessing rewarding social and family relationships, or being physically healthy, mentally alert, and emotionally stable—or all of these!

As you begin your journey within this book, there are stories, analogies, ideas, concepts, strategies, techniques, and action steps that will make you stop and go **hmmm**. Every chapter is independent, so feel free to jump around. Or you can focus on the topics that interest you most. Take your time, read a chapter or two, put the book down, think about what you've read—in other words, really give yourself some time to go "**hmmm**"—and then come back when you're ready for more. **Hmmm** comes quickly for some and slower for others, and your unique life experience and point of view will play a part in how **hmmm** happens for you in each chapter. The only rule I have for you is this: don't make this book an ornament or another collectable for your bookshelf. Tuck it into your briefcase, purse, or backpack and read it often because the **hmmm** in your life is as important as water and air. As you'll soon find, you need it to survive, thrive, and ultimately succeed.

Enjoy your hmmms!

"CHOOSE: When life throws unexpected curve balls your way, you can be bitter or better...you *choose!* You can be resentful or resilient...you *choose!* You can be distracted or disciplined...you *choose!* And ultimately, you can be a victim or victorious...you *choose!* CHOOSE WISELY!"

Hmmm #1

Thinking Three Moves Ahead

Have you ever paid attention to the value of a chess match before? While most people probably perceive chess as a boring, noncompetitive activity lacking intensity, that couldn't be further from the truth. Anyone who truly understands the game of chess clearly knows what it means to be a strong player, what it means to have complete concentration and focus, and what it means to be able to have total control in order to strategize, calculate, and make critical decisions in a mere matter of minutes—if not seconds. That's a skill that plays a major role in becoming a champion in the game of chess, no different from what's essential to becoming a champion in life.

Think about what is going through the minds of the two players sitting across from each other. The players aren't just thinking about the current move in front of them. They're thinking about all of the counter moves to their one move; "If I do this, what will my opponent do? And how will that affect my other moves? If I give up this pawn, will it put me in a position to capture their knight?" A good player sees the entire board—the big picture—and has an understanding of where each and every piece is on the board. Most importantly, a good player understands the effect that each move will have on everything else, not just this move but on future moves.

Hmmm—a lot like life . . . if you're doing it right. If you want to be successful, you have to think *at least* three moves ahead and you must have depth in your thinking. Now, that doesn't mean that everything you think, say, and do requires a wet suit and two scuba tanks to dive in deep to figure out. Some situations are just a small puddle, meaning they don't require much thought at all. But many things do require depth, focus, and strategy and ultimately require the skill of a chess player. You have to constantly think: "If I do this, what can happen? How will people react? What opportunity could this lead to?" The idea is not to just look at the immediate situation but to pull back and look at the whole picture. What are the advantages, upsides, and rewards or consequences, disadvantages, and risks of each of your actions? If you're not thinking three moves ahead in your life, your career, managing of people in your life, and your everyday encounters, then you're not being nearly as effective as you could be in the decisions you're making. And remember, every decision you make will affect the rest of your life.

In chess, you succeed by thinking every move through so that you ultimately place yourself in the strongest position and place your opponent in checkmate. In life, however, victory may not be always about beating an opponent. Sometimes it's helping other people to win so that you win too. It can be getting an employee or a team member to improve their performance so that they become a top achiever. They win with bonuses, financial freedom, and better reviews and recognition, and so do you, with a higher bottom line for your department or company or a stronger and more profitable business. Maybe it's getting your teenage son to drive safely and responsibly. He wins with a clean driving record and lower insurance, and so do you, with fewer gray hairs. Thinking several moves ahead helps you to enjoy more pleasure and less pain.

A big part of thinking ahead is making a risk/reward analysis. Let's use a simple example: drinking a lot. No big deal, right? I'm sure we've all seen instances of people throwing back several beers, drinking a bottle of wine (or two or three), or finishing off a handful of strong cocktails without ever considering how they're going to be perceived once they've crossed the point of no return or how they're going to feel the next morning when they need to function at a high level or, even worse, getting in their car and being pulled over by the police.

Imagine if this happened to you: The officer asks you to step out of the car, and soon he's giving you a breathalyzer test. You've gone from having a really good time to having a really bad time in one move—the move you didn't consider. Instead of going home to your own comfortable bed, you're going to sleep on a hard jailhouse floor. Inevitably, when you sober up, you'll be thinking, *Was that buzz worth it?* or *Why didn't I just call a cab?* Either way, you'll probably wish you thought three moves ahead before it ever got to that point. The pain of that decision won't just end when your hangover does; it will be with you as you face losing your license and possibly your livelihood, amongst many other painful repercussions.

To be clear, I'm not trying to come down on anyone who has a drink. I have an occasional beer or glass of wine myself, but I am just always thinking, *Is this a potential risk for me?* If so, it isn't worth it.

I also want to express how important this notion of thinking three moves ahead is in the context of good parenting. In other words, this is not just an exercise for adults to execute but something every parent should teach their kids as early as possible. This is a skill that can and will affect the rest of children's lives. Imagine the difference in the young student attending school who knows if they are respectful, well behaved, and attentive that they will create a positive identity for themselves that will lead to many advantages and even give them some leeway if they do make an ill-advised decision. However, on the flip side, if that same student misbehaves constantly, thereby creating a poor identity, they will often be looked upon as the guilty party when any situation arises. Imagine a college freshman attending a university on a full scholarship who, in a desire to fit in and without thinking three moves ahead, slips up with an impulsive inappropriate act and, because of it, loses the scholarship. Please, those of you who are parents, constantly remind your children to think three moves ahead—and explain why!

While some actions will have bigger consequences than others, it's a useful practice to start thinking three moves ahead in any situation. The idea is to always be thinking beyond the immediate situation, action, or problem you're facing. Now, let me clarify so there is no confusion—it is very important to live in the now; however, what we're talking about in this **hmmm** chapter is about our ongoing decision-making process. The depth in our thinking and our ability to think three moves ahead needs to be happening on a moment-by-moment basis. It needs to be a habit, something you don't even have to think about—automatic. It becomes what I call "subconscious competence." It's the idea that every decision or every move has a consequence or a counter move—large or small, good or bad. The better and faster you are at evaluating what you're doing and calculating the outcomes of each action, the more successful you will become in everything you do.

I'm at the point in my life where I consider most situations with this philosophy. My approach is very simple: it's all about results. Everything I say and do is all about considering what the upside is and what the downside is. So, even when it comes to the basics—like maintaining a positive attitude—it's not that I don't have problems or failures, it's that there is no upside to being negative or discouraged. There is only a downside, like losing an opportunity or a relationship, and why would I want that to be my end result? So being positive only has an upside and no downside. Simple, isn't it? Get in the habit of asking yourself, *What is the upside and what is the downside?* At first, until you get good, you might even have to take a sheet of paper, draw a line down the middle, and put upside on one side and downside on the other. See in print what makes the most sensible decision. Eventually, you'll be able to do this in your head in minutes and sometimes seconds.

There are so many instances where this philosophy is applicable. Take baseball, for instance. There is so much more to it than hitting a ball and running around the bases. It's a game in which thinking several moves ahead is vital to winning. The manager of each team is always tweaking the lineup and deciding on certain strategies for specific situations. "Do I tell the pitcher to walk their homerun hitter with two outs and runners on first and second?" "Whom do I bring in as my closer for this situation?" Each scenario has consequences tied to others; seeing the big picture is one of the most critical skills a successful manager must have.

In addition, players don't just run around the bases—they evaluate what they'll do depending on dozens of possible scenarios. The ball is hit in the air but they're looking at it and trying to decide if it's going to be caught—and, if they're good, they're almost to second by the time it is. A shortstop must already have possible outcomes worked out in his head—whether to throw the ball home and save a run or turn a double play—long before the ball meets the bat. Thinking three—or more!—moves ahead isn't specific only to baseball; it applies to every sport and everything.

While we may not be players or managers on a baseball field, we are definitely players and managers in our lives. We need to think ahead in every situation that counts and that's nearly every part of our life. You've got to do a certain amount of evaluation on everything. If I don't return someone's call in a timely fashion what may that person think of me? Maybe they don't want to do business with me. If I forget to wish one of my top performers a happy birthday, they may consider me unappreciative or ungrateful. Do I want that? Of course not, so I make sure to put their birthday on my calendar so I'll remember. Could I apologize for not doing it and offer belated birthday wishes? Sure, but it obviously wouldn't have the impact of actually thinking of that person and wishing them a happy birthday on time.

What if while things are good financially, I spend frivolously and don't save sensibly? If all of a sudden I lose my job or my business declines, I'm immediately facing financial challenges simply because I did not think three moves ahead.

Or how about having enough depth in your thinking to know when taking a secondary role will be in the best interest of everyone to achieve more? However, if you're not yet aware of thinking three moves ahead then your surface thinking wouldn't even have you consider not being the star for the sake of the show. *Pretty deep, huh?* Believe it or not, most people have very little depth in their thinking and that's why they find themselves in more unfortunate circumstances than are necessary.

Just constantly be aware of what your words and actions are going to be and what domino effect they're going to create because what you're about to do now will impact the next thing you do, and the next and the next. Everything you do, everything you say, and every action you take makes up an ever-expanding chain of causations.

As well-respected author Stephen Covey, a man I co-authored a book with, said, "While we are free to choose our actions, we are not free to choose the consequences of our actions." Once we've decided and made our move, the moves to follow are out of our hands. That's why it's critical to manage and control your risks by thinking three moves ahead. It's being aware. It's putting your ego aside to take good counsel, it's being as knowledgeable as possible, it's being patient, it's calculating and strategizing, it's seeing the whole picture, not just the move in front of you, but all the moves, on the greatest chess board of all: your life.

Hmmm #2

I Don't Care!

That's right, **I don't care.** I mean it!

Now don't get me wrong, I care about a lot of things and a lot of people. That's not what I'm referring to here. When I say I don't care, I mean I don't care what unqualified people think—and neither should you. Oh and by the way, most people are unqualified. I wouldn't be where I am today if I had listened to other people's opinions about what I should or shouldn't be doing. Unqualified people will always tell you with great authority that you can't change your life, start a new career, get a better job, start a business, think a different way, or do anything positive that deviates from what they consider the norm.

When I began thinking differently about success and got started in my own business, I was met with tremendous opposition. Everybody told me, "Gregg, you're crazy. This idea is crazy." People were telling me it (whatever *it* was) will never work. Here's a sampling of what I heard: "You don't know what you're doing." "How in the world do you think this could work?" "What makes you think you could succeed at this?" I'm sure you've heard similar words of discouragement when you made changes in your life or tried to take a different path. Years ago, my own family even made fun of me for what I was doing and the product I was selling. They told me I would never make any money. "Just look at how many other people have tried network marketing and failed!" they said. They told me I would fail too. I ignored the naysayers. I didn't care then and I don't care now.

To be successful, you must have a singular vision, thorough planning on where you want to go, and a focus on how you're going to get there. Listening to people say you can't make it will just prove them right. Get distracted by doubt and you'll fail for sure. When I started out, I wasn't interested in the people who had failed at my line of work. I listened to the people who had been successful. Is there really anyone else to listen to? A prime secret to success is not only what you know but, more importantly, who you got what you know from. Would you take financial advice from someone who's struggling financially? Or receive health care from a so-called doctor who didn't graduate from medical school? Or hand your car keys over to a mechanic who can't figure out how to open the hood? Yet many people do exactly that every day. They ask the guy at work (who still drives a Ford Pinto) whether they should invest in a particular stock. They listen intently when Cousin Vinny (who still lives in his mom's basement) presents his plan for peace in the Middle East. It's like asking someone who has never left town what vacationing in the south of France is like.

They don't have the knowledge or expertise to give an accurate answer. In the same way, the people who are saying you can't do this have no idea what it's really like because they've never done it either! So why are you asking them? More importantly, why are you listening when they protest you doing something they've never even tried?

At one time or another, we've all listened to other people's opinions about what we should do. I'm here to tell you that it's the single deadliest threat to your personal success. Most people don't talk *themselves* out of opportunities. Instead, they let *other people* do it. At the beginning of every venture there's always that doubt in the back of your mind. You're hearing that voice of fear—"No! Don't do it!" or "What if it doesn't work?" And you're hearing the optimistic voice—"Go ahead, make it happen!" or "What if it *does* work?" You're going back and forth and you aren't quite sure of yourself so you seek out approval and validation from others.

But that can be a huge mistake, depending on whom you ask. The only opinions I listen to are those coming from people with proven, documented results. The rest I don't care about. I may hear opinions all day but, unless they meet that criterion, I'm polite but I don't listen because **I Don't Care.**

The bottom line: don't let others keep you from doing the things that make you successful or even just happy. Some people may love to dance but they don't go dancing because they're worried that others might be watching and saying, "That guy has no rhythm." Who cares? Unless you're trying to become a professional, award-winning dancer like Fred

Astaire, why would that even matter? You're not auditioning for *Dancing with the Stars* so what weight does their opinion hold anyway? The opinions of others are irrelevant unless they're a professional dance instructor you hired because of your personal desire to become a better dancer. In that case, you'd better care what they have to say because you asked for it and they're qualified to give it.

However, if you love to dance just for fun but rarely hit the floor because you're afraid of what others will say, then it's time for *you* to say **"I Don't Care!"** When I'm out dancing with my wife, she runs circles around me. It would be easy for me to be self-conscious but **I Don't Care.** I'm just cutting loose, having a good time, and that's all that matters. Most of the time, opinions come from those who are too scared to even get out there on the dance floor themselves! People like that aren't going to keep me at home, not when I could be out having a good time.

If you look at the big picture, dancing is a strong metaphor for life. The key is that you have to dance. So tune out the dream snatchers and spirit crushers and tune in to your own music. Why? Because you have the **I Don't Care** attitude. It's impossible to silence all of the critics. Even the most successful people in the world who have already proven themselves over and over continuously face the know-it-alls, the critics, and the detractors. When you make it in the world, they still come after you. That will be true for the rest of your life. You might be a rock star with a score of gold albums and the critics will continue to say, "He can't do it. He's over the hill."

The Rolling Stones became one of the biggest musical groups of the 1960s, cutting one top ten album after another. Decades later, and in their sixties, they're still touring, still selling out stadiums, and playing for aging fans and their adult children. Lead singer Mick Jagger is still dancing across the stage as if he were twenty, belting out songs he wrote long before many of his listeners were even born. Rock bands aren't supposed to do that. Well, Mick and the boys just don't care.

Other greats throughout history had an **I Don't Care** attitude too. I think of Wilbur and Orville Wright, who were told, "If man were meant to fly, they would have had wings." The conventional wisdom of that time was that man would never be able to achieve the dream of flying. But the Wright brothers said to themselves, "We don't care," and the plane they invented soared—changing the world forever. The same was true for Martin Luther King Jr. and Rosa Parks, two of the most influential figures in the civil rights movement. Rosa Parks, a black woman, refused to give up her seat on the bus to a white passenger—even though it was against the law. She is remembered today as an icon. And what about Dr. King? On his rise to become one of the most celebrated social leaders of all time, his life was threatened because he refuted the notion that black people didn't deserve any of the basic civil liberties that whites had always been granted. Today, King's "I Have a Dream" speech is revered as one of the most powerful in history and he is remembered as one of the world's greatest leaders.

The greatest and most successful people in the world have all said, in one way or another, **I Don't Care**. They had a dream. They had a vision. They had the desire to follow through. And they didn't care about the obstacles in front of them or the criticisms they faced along the way.

They learned, as I've learned, that when someone tells you you're crazy to be doing whatever it is you're doing, you should be elated by it and thankful for it. When people tell me I'm crazy, I look them dead in the face, smile, and say thanks. "You just gave me the greatest compliment in the world. Can you say it again? Tell me I'm crazy." Their comment only means I'm on the right track because I'm just following in the footsteps of the greatest leaders and the most successful people. They were all called crazy before ultimately being called a genius. Thomas Edison, crazy to genius; Bill Gates, crazy to genius; Oprah Winfrey, crazy to genius. Can you think of anyone else? I'm sure scores of people. The funny part is all of those people wouldn't even consider themselves geniuses—nope, just average people with above average dreams, work ethic, commitment, follow through, persistence, and, most importantly, the **I Don't Care** attitude!

I love being a lunatic because I'm in great company. If you want to taste success then join us. When people called me crazy, they were trying to put out the small flame that was growing inside me. Instead, those words just poured gasoline on it and created a blaze that is still raging today. That blaze is called an "action motivator," and believe me, I've had my fair share. I recall one evening my uncle, a man who had many more years of professional sales experience than me, kept interrupting my sales presentation. After several unnecessary interjections, I literally had to ask him to leave, and as you might imagine, he was appalled and not very happy with me. As he turned to leave, he looked down at me (he's a couple of inches taller) and said, "You don't know anything about business—it will just be a matter of time before I say, 'I told you so!'" Well, to say that was a defining moment in my career would be an understatement because, in that brief instance, I had to decide if this was going to be a motivator or a de-motivator. I think it's clearly obvious which way I went; not only was I motivated, I was action motivated, meaning I set a goal and went to work. I remember getting back to my presentation and telling the audience, who by the way were predominately made up of strangers, that I would one day be driving a black with black interior 300E Mercedes Benz. I'm sure at that time they were probably thinking, *What is this guy talking about?* But **I Didn't Care** and I set my eye on the prize; sure enough, one day I had that exact car.

Now, you're probably thinking the first thing I did was bask in the glory of my achievement and immediately drive to my uncle's house to show him what I had accomplished. Not even close. The first thing I did was go to the Department of Motor Vehicles to get a custom tag that said "TOLDUSO." (I wanted to get something else but they wouldn't allow it—just kidding.) Now you may be thinking *then* I showed it to my uncle. Nope. I never showed it to him (he'll only know if he reads this book, shhh!). As a matter of fact, I thanked him because his actions moved me to achieve that goal. I didn't need to show him because his lack of awareness didn't warrant my revenge. No, this tag was for me, to remind me that if an unqualified person, no matter who they are, gives me an unqualified and unsolicited opinion, **I Don't Care.** As long as I believe I can then I will! So when somebody tries to put you down or gives you advice that's based on ignorance, tell them **"I Don't Care!"** When you're going through a tough time and that doubt is nagging at you, then say it out loud: **"I Don't Care."** When everything seems to be going against you, when the path to success seems too full of obstacles, when the chips are down and you feel like you can't go on, say it again: **"I Don't Care."** Yell it if you have to: **"I DON'T CARE!"** And if you're willing to make those three little words your constant mantra then watch out because your life will never be the same again!

Hmmm #3

Pros Make the Big Bucks

Ask yourself this: Are you a professional or an amateur? Are you playing at the big-league level or are you participating in a recreational activity? Do you view what you do as a profession or as a mere hobby? Now, there's no right or wrong, good or bad answer; it simply boils down to what you want your results to be. Because I assure you, if you're seeking financial independence, significant success, and personal fulfillment—you need to be nothing less than a pro!

By now, you might be thinking, *What is this guy talking about? Of course, I'm a professional.* Okay, if that's true, can you define what a professional is and describe what a professional does? Are you already stumped? Then maybe you're not a professional just yet! However, don't feel bad; most people really don't know what it means to be a true professional. There was certainly a time I didn't know either.

As kids, we grow up admiring professionals. As I mentioned earlier, I wanted to be a professional basketball player when I was a kid. It was my greatest passion. I played all the time. I recall coming home from school, dropping my books, grabbing my ball, running to the park, and literally shooting hoops 'till the sun went down. On many of those evenings, my mom was pretty annoyed with me because I was late coming home for dinner.

I was considered pretty good but compared to what? The rest of the neighborhood kids. Ultimately, I played a little college ball but that's where my basketball career ended. I wanted desperately to take it further but I was missing two critical elements and they work hand-in-hand to make the difference—and no, it wasn't a couple of feet in height and few pounds in weight. **I didn't have a reference point**, and therefore **I didn't have a professional's mindset and skill set.** I never really knew what it took to become a professional basketball player.

Think about it—who was my coach, who was my mentor, who gave me a road map of what it actually takes to be a professional basketball player? You guessed it—I relied on *my own* thoughts and ideas. Sure, I had some coaches along the way but they didn't have a big-league reference point either. So as I look back, I realize now that unless you're a natural (which I was not), a reference point and the right mindset and skill set are absolute necessities for you to be a pro.

Lebron James, the professional basketball phenom, is a great example of a natural. Of course, he had plenty of guidance along the way and, of course, he worked hard. But give me a break: I think he was born six foot eight, 250 pounds, primed for the NBA. Not to take anything away from Lebron, but some people just got it like that—destined from the start for a certain career.

For me, it took many years to figure out what my professional passion was, and now I'm doing it. If you're still searching for yours, or just trying to go from amateur to professional, I really believe these **hmmms** will help you.

So, it's safe to say that we all want to be professionals at what we do. We see that pros have the greatest success. We see the big money being made by those in the big leagues who have mastered their game, whether they're baseball pitchers, heart surgeons, entrepreneurs, entertainers, executives, or financial managers.

Some of those people who've made it to the top of their field had an advantage because of parents who paved the way. Think of Payton Manning and his brother Eli who are currently Super Bowl winning quarterbacks in the NFL. They are the sons of another great professional quarterback, Archie Manning. Kobe Bryant, the great NBA basketball player, is the son of an NBA player, too. Tiger Woods' dad, Earl, was an avid golfer. He served as a coach and mentor to his son, teaching him mental conditioning techniques that would come in handy when Tiger entered the high-pressure world of professional golf.

Then there's the Hollywood crowd: Elvis Presley and daughter Priscilla. Gwyneth Paltrow and Kate Hudson, whose mothers are standout actresses Blythe Danner and Goldie Hawn, respectively. Father-and-son actors Kirk and Michael Douglas. Musician Jacob Dylan, whose father is the legendary Bob Dylan. Patti Duke and Shawn Austin. Billy Ray Cyrus and daughter Miley, who made it big on Disney. And this list could go on forever.

The same is true in business. Think about how many individuals who come from successful families also end up successful or how many times there are several doctors in the same family. These parents provided their children with a reference point of what it takes to be a professional. I didn't have that benefit. Of course, my parents wanted the best for me but they didn't know what it would take for me to realize my dream. They couldn't provide me with the blueprint I needed to be a professional basketball player.

And it wasn't that I couldn't have been an NBA basketball player if I had done the right things. There are a few six-foot-two, slow, white basketball players who have made it big. (John Stockton is one of them.) It can be done, but only if you do all the right things in the right way. I didn't have that knowledge, and as a result, I always had an amateur mentality, not the professional mindset and skill set that makes success in the big leagues possible.

So this is an important **hmmm**: to be a professional you must have a reference point, whether that is in sports or your particular industry, becoming wealthy, or any other endeavor that you're trying to achieve greatness in. And you must understand what it takes to perform at that level—the mindset and skill set necessary. You must respect what it means to think and act in a professional manner every time you perform or play your game.

This mindset is critical to reach the top levels of any profession or activity, and it isn't limited to pro sports figures. If I asked an audience of thousands of people if they wanted to be financially independent, I'd bet that every single person would raise his or her hand. Nobody would say, "No, not me." Everybody would say, "Yes, I want that!"

It's easy to raise your hand and say, "Yes, I want it!" but getting to that point is another story entirely. Becoming financially independent requires an incredible amount of work. It demands that you do certain things over and over again and that you do them in the right way. It demands discipline. It requires that you learn not only how to make money but how to handle and invest money. It's hard work!

And out of all those people who raise their hands, how many actually do what it takes to reach that goal? Sadly, not many. Few have a true understanding of what's necessary to be financially independent and successful.

Let's take it one step further and assume you want to be a millionaire—who doesn't? But what's your reference point to get there? Do you spend time with other millionaires? Have you observed business people starting from scratch and then building fortunes? True success comes to a very small number of individuals and only a small percentage reach the lofty millionaire status. Similarly, millions of people play basketball just like I did. Hundreds of thousands of kids dream of being like their professional idols but there are only 360 players currently on NBA rosters. Do you realize what an achievement it is to make it into pro sports? Do you understand the magnitude of that accomplishment? That mentality, skill, and tenacity to make it a reality are what separate a pro from an amateur.

The professional understands what's at stake and knows exactly what's needed to succeed. It's not a guessing game; it's an exact science. It's gaining that reference point, converting it into a game plan, and then implementing it. Are you ready for that? Then pay close attention because listed below are the five keys to becoming a professional.

Key Number 1—Love for the Game!

You've got to be passionate about the game you're playing. You really have to love what you're doing because with love comes determination, focus, desire, and commitment. Sports are a great example. You can watch athletes who love their sport and, because of that love, they go to the greatest lengths to win. That mentality is applicable to every area of your life. Whether it's in business, career, finances, or how you raise your family, you need to make a decision. Are you going to do what it takes to be a professional and experience the life of a champion or are you going to sit in the stands as an amateur and miss the chance to win big?

Of course, being a pro is a substantial challenge, and you have to know upfront that you'll face rejection, adversity, and setbacks. However, if you have the passion for your game, you'll accept these things as just part of the process to achieving your goals, knowing you'll eventually come out on top.

Think about professional baseball players. They know statistically that the odds are stacked against them. No one in the history of the game has ever batted a .1000 in one season, or ever batted .900 or .800 or .700 or .600 or even .500, and only a couple of players have ever batted .400. And no one has ever done it for an entire career. Nevertheless, a true pro baseball player steps into that batter's box expecting to get a hit every time, visualizing success. The love of the game creates the professionalism to be prepared, to have positive expectations, and to envision a successful outcome. If players don't get a hit, meaning they experienced a short-term failure, what do they do? Cry? Whine? Make excuses? Hardly! They run back to the dugout and consider what they can take from that experience to gear up for their next opportunity.

On the flip side, what would the amateur do? Probably be disappointed and discouraged and maybe even reevaluate their decision to have played the game in the first place. That's why you have to love the game you're playing because your love won't let you give up. It will drive you and all those failures and setbacks will only make winning that much sweeter!

Key Number 2—Coaching and Mentoring!

Professionals have coaches and mentors because they're not going to leave anything to chance. There must be a pretty good reason for the best of the best to see value in coaching. Whether they're athletes, singers, movie stars, business owners, or high-level executives, these individuals have coaches—people they turn to who have expertise in that area. Coaches see things from an objective viewpoint and can offer a fresh perspective. It's simple—if professionals have coaches and mentors, shouldn't an amateur striving to become a professional expect to have one? As a matter of fact, doesn't the amateur really need it more than the professional, considering he or she hasn't even gotten there yet?

I've realized this since the day I started on my road to change. As an entrepreneur, I've had coaches and mentors and, even now, as a professional, I still have coaches and mentors. The fact is I will always have them in my life because I'm never going to know enough. I also want someone to hold me accountable and keep me on track to help me fulfill my true potential. The reality is that most of us just function better and achieve more when we are encouraged, guided, and held to a certain standard. And if each of us is honest with ourselves, we can look back at a time in our lives where someone played a significant role in our ability to excel. Maybe it was our parents, teachers, family members, coaches, or a distant relative, but they pushed us to be better than we were. So we need to place ourselves in that same circumstance to once again be pushed to be the best.

Key Number 3—Consistent Practice!

A pro practices day after day to perfect their skills. An amateur just plays the games. Most people want professional results but treat the game like a hobby. Practice is one of the most crucial elements of performance, and that's why pros do it. Yet, to amateurs it's not nearly as important, even though practice is the major difference between amateurs and professionals.

I'll give you a great example of how this applies in my own life. As I already mentioned, I love to play basketball, and I still play in a recreational basketball league. Now, of course, we're just playing for a little fun and exercise and we certainly don't have practices; we just get out there and play the game. But the key is that I'm aware enough to know that all I can be in basketball is an amateur, and I'm happy with that. However, in other areas of my life, I choose to be a professional. I, therefore, act accordingly and consistently practice the mindset and skill set required of me to achieve excellence.

The point I'm making is that it's okay to be an amateur at something as long as you made the choice to treat it that way and it makes you happy. But, if you have ideas of being a professional in certain areas of your life, then you must be diligent in your practice.

Referring back to baseball, let's take an individual like Derek Jeter, a famous and successful perennial all-star who played for the world-renowned New York Yankees. He is a player who has made over $20 million a year and is considered one of the game's best all-around players, and you know what? *He still practices!* So here's a guy who's obviously great at fielding ground balls and hitting a baseball but, every year when spring training opens, he's right out there going through a rigorous regimen of fielding grounder after grounder in addition to hitting ball after ball at batting practice. When the season starts, you'll find him out before every game taking more grounders. Then, what does he do between every inning? Takes more ground balls! In fact, Jeter—like so many other highly paid professionals—never stops practicing. No matter how many times he executes a play, he comes right back and does it again. He's always working to get better, to stay among the best.

Why? Because pros understand that practicing something the right way is critical to making it a habit in your subconscious mind, thereby making it instinctive. Oh, and let's not forget that Jeter is already a pro, so how much more and how much harder did he practice to actually become a pro?

Of course, practice isn't limited to big-league sports. You have to practice in order to master any skill, including those that make for a successful salesperson, business owner, or leader. As a speaker, trainer, salesman, and leader, I practice. That means I often do pertinent exercises by myself or stand in a room by myself and practice my presentations. I stand in front of other people who assess me. I repeat these presentations over and over again until they're not just better, they're as perfect as I can make them. I want passionately to be a pro not an amateur.

Why spend so much time practicing? Athletes know there are always other players waiting to take their place. If they falter or don't keep up, then someone better will push them aside. They're always practicing because they know their competitors are doing the same thing. Their opponents are always getting better and they better be too, unless they want to see their starting spot lost and their contract cut by millions next year. The great NBA Hall of Famer Ed Macauley put it this way: "When you are not practicing, remember, someone somewhere is practicing, and when you meet him he will win."

Another important factor in regards to practice is dispelling the myth that *practice makes perfect* because in reality, *practice makes permanent.* If you practice the wrong things, you're going to be really good at doing them wrong. You have to make sure you're practicing the right things so that the permanent habits you're creating are the ones that will lead to the results you want.

There's another reason professionals constantly practice: so they can perform at their highest level even if they're not competing against someone else. Think about entertainers. Imagine going to a concert performed by Celine Dion, and while you sit there in awe of the event, you're not even realizing that for every minute spent on stage, she spent hours and hours practicing and rehearsing. She doesn't just get up on stage with dozens of dancers, ten outfit changes, twenty songs with complex choreography, and—boom!—her concert just comes together out of thin air. She practices for hours and hours to be the very best.

The fans sit there and applaud and think, *They make it look so easy!* Those fans have no reference point for what it takes to produce that kind of performance. They see the finished product and maybe they vaguely realize that it takes a lot of work, but it's not a clear, concise vision. It's hard for them to have the appropriate respect for what it really took because they haven't seen it and they haven't experienced it. Wow! That's a great **hmmm**! You see, most people don't have respect for how hard it is to achieve financial independence or anything that produces high levels of success. Most people don't have the appropriate amount of respect for how dedicated you must be and the type of consistent commitment you must have over a long period of time. Do you think Derek Jeter became as great as he is overnight? I'm sure he would tell you a different story. He had respect and love for the game and put in the time and energy to get that great.

On Sundays when you watch pro football on TV, you see the game but you don't see the five or six days of long, grueling practice that preceded it. Every one of the players, from the quarterback to the offensive tackle to the place kicker, has spent hours every day getting ready for what they will do on that one Sunday.

That's the biggest difference between the amateur and the professional—amateurs just perform. An amateur salesperson goes on a sales call totally unrehearsed and does a presentation without first practicing it. A professional salesperson practices his or her sales presentation and overcoming objections. In life, a true professional practices what he or she is going to say, studies and learns how to raise a family, how to communicate with others, how to be a good leader, how to make and manage money. A professional is well equipped and prepared for making decisions. And, if you spend the time learning and practicing what you learn, then you'll make better choices and better decisions, which will contribute significantly to the outcome of your life.

Key Number 4—The Sacrifice (which I like to call the investment)!

The reason I believe the meaning of sacrifice in this context is really an investment is because a sacrifice usually refers to some type of loss. But in most cases when you're striving for success, whatever it is you're committing (energy, money, time), once you hit your goal, it generally gives you your success plus your original investment back. Just a **hmmm** to consider.

For some reason, baseball is on my mind and a big part of this **hmmm**. But I believe this sport is an excellent example of highlighting this key to being a pro. My good friend Dave Parker, who played Major League Baseball for nearly twenty years, was a successful player. He was a seven-time All-Star, a batting champion, a Gold Glove winner, an MVP, and a two-time World Series Champion. But to me, what he exemplifies most about being a true professional is the personal sacrifice he made to become a pro and, ultimately, a champion.

Dave has told me stories of how he spent eleven months a year for five consecutive years playing baseball. Literally, after the season was over here in the States, he would travel to another country and play over there. There were plenty of hard times while he was in the minor leagues, like when he couldn't even afford to pay his power bill and lived in the dark for several days at a time. Would you be willing to make that kind of investment, that type of sacrifice? Dave was willing to put it all on the line; he was willing to make the investment. In the end, he got everything back that he put in by achieving tremendous financial and personal success.

There are innumerable people out there who have achieved greatness through their willingness to put forth what most people won't even consider—making that investment. That's what you've got to do with your life. You have to invest in yourself because *you're the best investment you've got!*

Key Number 5—Always Be Ready!

Not get ready—be ready! In most games, an amateur is often not ready. Think about a recreational softball game. Perhaps the right fielder is in the outfield and she's looking up in the stands, waving at her boyfriend, and not paying attention to the game. She's distracted because she's not getting much action. But when she least expects it, the ball is going to come flying past her, or she's going to get whacked in the head because she wasn't paying attention. That's an amateur: a person who will miss a prime opportunity to shine because they weren't ready. They weren't prepared. They weren't poised to put everything they practiced into action.

And that's the final piece to being a pro and for achieving success in general—YOU **MUST BE READY!**

And if you're not ready in your professional endeavors, you're poised to miss out big-time. Next time you get the chance, pay attention to a pro baseball player's every move—they're always down in their stance, ready on every pitch of every inning of every game. The left fielder isn't saying to himself, "I hardly ever get a ball hit to me, so I think I'm going to lie down for a while and take it easy." Or how about in football—does the wide receiver stop running routes because the quarterback hasn't thrown him the ball in a while? Of course not, just like the salesperson doesn't stop presenting because the last five prospects weren't interested. Parents don't stop parenting because their kids haven't responded the way they've wanted them to. Why? Because they're pros! And pros are always ready!

And the pro is ready with the same level of focus, intensity, and desire each and every time, no matter how many games they've played. Each and every time they hit a home run it's just as exciting for them as the first time. Think about those Cirque du Soleil performers. What consummate pros. They have the daunting task of performing the same acts over and over and over again. Day after day and city after city. Yet, they display the same passion, enthusiasm, and energy each and every time. Why? Because they're pros. They're ready to provide a great show for the audience, even though they've done the show hundreds of times.

A professional recognizes that even though the job requires doing the same things over and over again, the audience is always different. A professional has the ability to rise above human nature and has the discipline to be ready to perform. A true professional can perform night after night and year after year and muster the same passion each time and can do it passionately even in the face of losing.

Consider again Archie Manning, the great NFL quarterback I mentioned earlier. He was a fantastic player at Ole Miss. In the very first nationally televised college game, he threw for 436 yards and three touchdowns and rushed for 104 yards in a heartbreaking 33–32 loss to Alabama. He went on to play for the New Orleans Saints when they were a truly dreadful team, better known as the New Orleans "Ain'ts." Fans showed up to the games wearing paper bags over their heads so they wouldn't be recognized as supporting this awful team. Yet, even in the face of such adversity, Manning went out each Sunday and set records for passing and rushing—often running away from opposing tacklers who broke through what was the smallest offensive line in the league. Manning might have been playing on a losing team but he always played like a winner, giving everything he had to the game.

That's one of the most powerful attributes of being a professional—*always* being on your game—no matter what. Can you imagine a physician not being a true professional? That wouldn't be very promising for the patient lying there on the operating table. "Well, Mr. Jones, I'm just not feeling it today.

I'm not on my game. I removed the wrong organ. Sorry about that."

Now, that doesn't mean surgeons or any other professional for that matter are always going to be perfect. No one is. Things happen. Mistakes happen. You miss shots. Sometimes you screw up. But the point is that the mindset of a professional is, "I'll do everything I can to make sure I'm on my game today."

So that bears the question, are you on your game? Because now you have a reference point and you know the five keys to the right mindset and skill set to being a professional. **Hmmm**, are you willing to do what it takes to get that great? What if it took five years? How about ten? It shouldn't matter how long it takes, if you really want to be a pro!

This brings us back to what you're looking for most: tangible results of professionalism, like the money, the success, and the personal satisfaction of being the best. In the end, pros get *paid* the big bucks while amateurs *pay* the big bucks. The amateurs are the fans. They buy the tickets that pay the stars' salaries. And while there's nothing wrong with being a fan in the stands, if you want what the pros have, you have to get out of the stands and give everything you've got to play the greatest game of all—whatever your chosen game is!

"LIVE: Have you ever noticed that 'live' and 'live' are spelled the same, even though they mean two different things? Well if you 'live' your life like you were 'live' on Broadway, your life would be an amazing show, wouldn't it? *Live Life Live!"*

Hmmm #4

How Much Sand is Left in Your Hourglass?

From time to time, I wonder what it would be like to have the opportunity to sit down and interview God. One of my first questions would be: "Why do most people misuse, squander, and take for granted the most valuable and limited resource they have—time?"

Have you ever really thought about the concept of time? It's the one thing that we can never, ever get back. You can make a tremendous amount of money and then lose it all, only to gain it back and then some. The same goes with any physical possession, whether it's a house, a car, or a work of art—ultimately, it can be replaced. I know you may be thinking, *Those things may have sentimental value and if I lost them it would be a terrible loss.* Granted, that's true—but those things can be replaced, sometimes even with something better. You can even lose a friend or a loved one and still have the capacity to find new friends or find love again.

Time, however, doesn't work that way. It's a commodity that's absolutely irreplaceable—a concept that so many people completely fail to grasp. Once it's gone, it's gone. Yet, if you're like most people, you treat your time as if it was an unlimited resource. You act as if it's never going to run out: "Well, I didn't get much done today. No big deal. I'll make up for it tomorrow!"

But how do you know that for sure? There are no guarantees in life, and certainly one of the biggest is the fact that we can be here one day and gone the next.

So here's how each of us should view the most precious resource we have. Imagine that when you were born, as you took your first breath of life, simultaneously an hourglass appeared and it was immediately turned over, signifying the beginning of your life. What if this hourglass literally began to hover right beside you as the sand started to run slowly but steadily through the little hole in the middle leading to the bottom? It would mark the first day of the rest of your life. This hourglass would be your true measure of time.

As you'd begin to grow up, you would learn about your personal hourglass and what it represents. You'd soon realize that as each grain of sand slips through into the bottom of the hourglass, a part of your life is gone forever. No getting it back. But you'd also realize that everybody else has an hourglass hovering beside them as well. It's there twenty-four hours a day, seven days a week. It's sitting next to you while you eat, it's in the car as you drive, it's on the nightstand while you sleep, it runs with you, walks with you, bikes with you—you can't escape it. The sand is trickling away as you're reading these lines. The grains never stop passing—and the pace never slows. The grains of sands never stop . . . until you do.

With an hourglass marking your every second on Earth, you'd constantly keep an eye on it, wouldn't you? You'd think to yourself, "There goes my life. I can literally see how much time I have left." Stop right now and as you look at your hourglass, ask yourself these questions. How much more urgent should you be living your life? How seriously do you value this precious and extremely scarce resource? How many more times would you pick up the phone or visit with people just to say you loved them? How much more time would you spend with your children? How much less time would you spend worrying about what other people think? How many more chances, risks, and adventures would you take and enjoy? And, most importantly, how much less would you put off for tomorrow what you could have done today?

What if you had that physical hourglass? You'd live your life in a completely different way, wouldn't you?

Now, let's return to partial reality—because none of us has a physical hourglass to look at every day and, because we don't see it, we tend to take our sands of time for granted. But everyone does have an hourglass—it's just invisible! You can't see it, but believe me—it's there. Of course, our hourglasses are different sizes, because everyone has a different amount of sand left. I don't know how many grains you have left. I don't know how many I have. But let me tell you what I'm doing with them. I'm only doing things I love, spending as much time as I can with people I really want to be with, and doing the things that make me happy. I don't have time to settle, time to work somewhere I don't want to be, or time to spend with people I don't want to see. But mostly, I have no time to worry or stress about what I can't control. I'm dedicated to pouring my heart and soul into the things that are really important to me. I'm living my life as if that physical hourglass is hovering right there next to me. I can see it clear as day. And I'm making the best use of every grain I have left—however many or few there may be. I don't know when my time is going to be up. Maybe I only have a day's worth of sand left. Maybe I have fifty years—I have no clue—but I'm going to make absolutely sure that I use every grain. I have no excuses, only reasons because my life is passing by right before my eyes.

And just how valuable are those grains that are slipping away? Well, let's consider them from several perspectives. The grains in your hourglass are the essence of your life. You have no control over the fact that they're slipping away but you have absolute control over what you'll do with them before they do.

The hourglass changes the way you live your life. You're not going to procrastinate. You're not going to have complacency. You're not going to waste time. That confirmation of your life's passing is going to make you move. It's going to make you want to experience more while you still can. You're not going to keep saying, "Hey, why not put it off until tomorrow?" If you knew how much sand you had left, boy, you'd be doing things differently. You'd have a greater appreciation for so much more. The TV would be off and your family, your wife, your kids, your friends, your passions, your hobbies, or whatever fulfills you would be front and center. You'd have a greater work ethic than ever before. You'd get more done and focus on what really matters. You'd stop saving just for a rainy day and start living while the sun shines bright and clear.

Unfortunately, we don't have that ever-present view of our lives and how much time we have left. But what if we could simulate that visual reminder? Would you be interested in knowing how? It's simple, so let me share it with you. I began using this technique many years ago. I purchased a large elegant hourglass of my own. It currently sits in my china cabinet at home and every so often when I feel time slipping away, when I know I'm procrastinating or wasting time, I take it out and turn it upside down as a strong reminder that my time is moving. Get one for yourself and put it on your nightstand for a while. Every now and then turn it over and watch the sand fall and realize it represents your life passing before you each and every day.

It will be a reminder, a confirmation that time is never an unlimited resource. It's not like air. It's not like water. It can run out. It *will* run out! Time is not standing still—and neither should you. Resolve today that you're going to start seeing that virtual hourglass every day and develop a sense of urgency for right now. There's a well-worn cliché that says, "Time waits for no man." Nothing could be truer. Our lives are composed of a finite number of minutes, hours, days, weeks, and years. How will you use them?

So decide right now that you're living with a realization of the incredible value of time and then decide how you want to spend it. Stop making the excuse, "I would do it if I had time." As H. Jackson Brown, Jr., author of *Life's Little Instruction Book*, put it: "Don't say that you don't have enough time. You have exactly the same number of hours per day that were given to Helen Keller, Pasteur, Michelangelo, Mother Teresa, Leonardo da Vinci, Thomas Jefferson, and Albert Einstein."

You always have time for the things you really want to do. Ask yourself what it is you value and then see if you're putting your time into the activities, people, and circumstances that will reap the greatest rewards for you. And, when you need extra motivation, visualize that hourglass hovering beside you, its sands slipping away.

Hmmm #5

We're All Just "Big" Kids

The funniest part about kids is they want to be adults as quickly as possible; the funniest part about adults is they wish they were kids again. I believe a compromise is in order here. The way I see it, if we could continue to have the same drive, enthusiasm, resilience, energy, determination, curiosity, desire to learn, and fearlessness that we had as children and we could have kept those as we grew to become adults, we would have the best of both worlds and far greater success.

In many ways, we left most of what we needed to be immensely successful behind. You see, as kids, the majority of us didn't focus on making money because that was pretty much handled for us, but, believe it or not, we had the mindset of a millionaire way back then. Unfortunately, we were taught to grow up, to stop playing with toys, to stop playing hide and seek and make believe. But no one ever told us we would never stop being kids. Of course, we get bigger (some of us a lot bigger!) but our emotional needs never really change. It would be great if everyone understood that we all still have the same emotional needs we once had as kids. Unfortunately, in our efforts to become adults, we've lost the tremendous edge we once had as children.

Why is it that when we're kids and we talk about what is considered unrealistic as adults, we are patted on the head and encouraged? We might say we're going to be a professional athlete or an astronaut or a singer, and the adults around us might say, "Oh that's so cool," or "That's great! Anything is possible." But often, as soon as we reach high school and move towards our adulthood, it's more like, "When are you going to be realistic? Dreams are great but they don't pay the bills." At the same time, much of the consistent recognition, acknowledgment, and genuine and sincere celebration of our accomplishments are reduced down to an occasional "Good job."

If you recall, as small children, everything we did was a big deal: rolling over, our first step, walking, feeding ourselves, being potty trained, and on and on. These are monumental things, enough for our families to stop whatever they are doing to take pictures and shoot video of these events. Why did these expressions of praise lessen? Is it because our loved ones no longer thought we were worthy of praise, because they didn't find us as cute anymore, or because they didn't love us as much? No, it's because they were busy thinking of other things and because, honestly, they believed that we only needed that acknowledgment when we were small kids. We are much more mature now; therefore, they didn't think we needed it anymore.

So, is it true that once we grow to be mature adults we no longer have these particular emotional needs? No, it's not true; as a matter of fact, it is completely FALSE! As adults, we have the same emotional needs we once had as children except now we've just learned to pretend like we don't need it. For most of us, we get better at controlling our emotions so we usually don't start bawling when we don't get what we want or when someone doesn't praise us. And we probably won't throw a temper tantrum when someone tells us no. Well, at least most of us, because we all know some people who seem to have not done any growing up at all. We've all seen things that led us to say something like, "Wow, he hasn't grown up at all," or "She's acting like a five-year-old," or "They are so immature." We all know people that will do anything for recognition; they have to let you know they did a good job just to fulfill that fix of emotional security.

But those are more of the exceptions. Most of us are able to hold it together and at least look and sound like we're adults. We put on a politically correct appearance that tells society we've given up childish things and are in control of our emotions, our thoughts, our actions, and our lives. But on the inside, it's sometimes a very different story. Deep down, our emotional needs are still much the same as they were when we were children. You can pretend that you don't have them but they're still there waiting to be met. So how do we learn to tap into this emotional power that each of us possesses instead of falling prey to the insecurities that drive us to create a false façade of who we really are?

It starts with understanding one of the greatest emotional needs we all have: the need for acceptance and approval. For most of us, we greatly desire to be included in the group or be a part of the team or fit in at the office or just be in the "in crowd." We always feel better when people accept us and like what we're doing, what we're wearing, or where we're going. If that weren't true, there would be no need for "name brands," fashion, or status. Isn't it true that fashion, status, and what is considered to be the "in" thing is based upon what the majority of society dictates it is? Why are brands like Ralph Lauren, Coach, and Mercedes a big deal? Why do we wear a particular sports team logo on our hat or sweatshirt? If we weren't seeking approval and acceptance, we wouldn't care what the brands were or about proudly displaying our favorite teams on our clothing. But, you see, it's what gives us a sense of identity, a sense of being acknowledged. We crave the opportunity to be included and maybe even admired. We come alive when we're recognized and we love to be appreciated.

Think about it—and this is just a very simple example— how many times have we all tried on a pair of jeans or some other outfit and then asked your friend or spouse, "So, what do you think?" Now, mind you, this particular person may have no style or fashion sense at all but it's just our natural instinct to get someone to say, "Hey, it looks great." And in that moment, we feel good because our need for appreciation, recognition, inclusion, and, most importantly, our need to be loved is one of the greatest motivations we have.

You know, it's amazing how many people believe that money is the greatest motivator of all. And of course, it's true that people will work very hard for money, but they'll go to even greater lengths for pride and recognition, especially when those things are coming from individuals who are most important to them. Remember, we're talking about kids here who are simply disguised as adults. Once again, as kids, we weren't thinking of money, we were too busy being concerned about fitting in. We're still kids, just bigger! This is a good time to go **hmmm!**

To make this **hmmm** crystal clear, consider the following. For those of you who have children, the following task will be easy, and for those of you who don't, make it a point to spend just a few minutes observing the interaction between a child and parent. It won't take long for you to realize how powerful this **hmmm** is and how understanding it can change not only your financial position but your life. One of the simplest yet most powerful marketing philosophies says to find a need and fill it. Well, let me share a secret with you: everyone needs recognition, appreciation, and acceptance, and I will prove it by three of the greatest lessons I have ever been taught by three of the greatest teachers—my own children, Kellen, Kaleigh, and Kolten.

It was summertime, and I took Kellen to the pool, I got comfortable in a lounge chair and began reading a book. Kellen instantly got in the water and began swimming and playing around. But it wasn't long before he was standing at the side of the pool, looking at me, and calling out, "Daddy,

Daddy, Daddy, watch me jump in the pool!" So I put the book in my lap and looked at him with a big smile as he jumped in. As soon as his head came out of the water, he excitedly asked, "Did you see? Did you see?"

I said, "Yes, that was great!" And that was the end of my reading for a while.

He gave me a big grin and then said, "Watch me while I do it again!" For the next thirty minutes or so, this was the routine. And each and every time he waited with bated breath for me to smile and tell him, "That was great, son!"

My daughter Kaleigh is no different; whenever I attend one of her dance or gymnastics classes, she spends a majority of her time looking at me to make sure I'm watching her. As soon as the class is over she runs over to me to ask, "Did you see how I was dancing?" or "Did you see me tumbling?" It's so cute but it's also eye opening.

And we can't leave my son Kolten out, who reminds me to video record how he can shoot the ball into a regulation-size basketball hoop. The only problem is he spends so much time looking at me to make sure I'm watching him that he doesn't even look where he is shooting. And whenever he makes a basket, because I acknowledged his success with applause and accolades, he can't move fast enough to chase the ball down and repeat that action over and over and over again. Classic!

You see, kids aren't usually shy about asking for attention, just as my children and I'm sure your children prove during their activities. They'll even demand it by telling you, "Watch me! Watch me! Watch me!" or "Look at what I'm doing!" or "See what I made in school!" over and over again. That's what kids do. They haven't been conditioned yet to be a little more discreet or tactful about fulfilling their own emotional needs, and they're certainly not worried about what people think. They're just quenching their instinctive thirst to be recognized and acknowledged.

But as they get older, this outward demand for attention becomes a little more subtle as this well-adjusted child begins to develop self-confidence, self-appreciation, and a sense of security. Eventually, it's likely that kids will stop asking their loved ones to watch their every move but it doesn't mean those emotional needs don't still need to be met. Of course, the more we lack that self-confidence, self-appreciation, and sense of security, the more in need we are of approval. We all can relate to examples of teenagers scoring well on an exam, making a school sports team, getting a part in a school play, or getting accepted into college and wanting to tell anyone that would listen. Why? Because it feels good to share accomplishments and feels even better when people we care about are proud of us. On the flip side, we've also seen or heard stories of teenagers who gain attention by misbehaving and causing trouble. There is no denying we're going to get attention however we can.

As adults, we're supposed to be much more mature so we'd be pretty reluctant to just come right out and ask for approval, but often we'll be creative and inventive to find ways to get that recognition we desire. There are also people who will insist that they don't need to be recognized but usually that's not the whole truth, and in many cases, those are the people who require it most. Think about the fact that there are millions of people sitting at their desks or standing behind the counter at a store or on an assembly line or providing service for a company, department, or organization or building a business or being on a team—many of whom are saying to themselves, "Nobody appreciates me." They're doing their jobs every day or filling their role or just being a team player, and they're thinking, *Nobody ever notices my dedication or good work or the simple fact that I'm loyal, committed, and giving it my very best.*

When I speak to business owners, corporate executives, company managers, and organizational leaders, many times their assumption is that the number one complaint their employees and members will have is that they don't make enough money. Now, while that may be true and while those employees or team members may even be underpaid, usually what I find when I talk to these same people is that it's not so much about the money as it is about feeling unappreciated for the contribution they bring to the job, team, or organization. They don't feel recognized. They're standing on the edge of the pool, they're in dance class, they're shooting the ball in the basket, they're crying out, "Watch me, watch me!" But nobody's there to say "Great job!"

I can tell you that if your motivational strategy is to focus solely on the financial gain someone receives, don't expect the majority of your people to be with you long-term. That philosophy will lead mostly to a high turnover rate and costly attrition. Here's why: If the only thing that matters is the money, how much will it take to make someone happy? You see, for the most part it will never be enough, and if it doesn't live up to their expectations, you've got nothing else meaningful keeping them there. There is no emotional fulfillment, no reason to say, "You know what, I really like being a part of this team. I think I'm going to stick around." But if it's all about the money, it won't be long before the individuals who are not making money decide they feel better not being a part of your company or organization. That's why I constantly remind people that if you focus on money and only money, many times it will just elude you. But if you focus on intangibles such as personal growth, self-development, and the expression of gratitude and giving, you'd be amazed how much more loyalty and longevity your organization would sustain, not to mention how much more effort someone would give. And everybody wins in that case.

So the bottom line is, whether it's adults working in a corporate environment, building a business, or being on a team, people aren't going to tell you, "Hey, give me some recognition. I really need it right now." I think we'd all agree that would sound pretty childish. Can you imagine running up to your boss or, at a big event, charging up to the event leader and yelling, "Hey, look at me, I'm doing a good job, I'm giving a great effort." It just doesn't fit with a grown-up façade we all work so hard to maintain. Can you picture a forty-year-old person in a business suit bursting into their supervisor's office and shouting, "I'm finished, I did it exactly how you wanted! Now where is my pat on the back?" If that happened, the supervisor would likely make a quick call to Human Resources and say, "Umm, do we still do those psychological evaluations? I might need to set one up for Bob." (Or, even worse, he might start thinking about moving Bob to another department where another supervisor would have to deal with him.)

What so many business owners, executives, managers, and leaders tend to forget is that, although their employees, members, or colleagues are adults, they are still just kids in need of their approval and praise. This is the key to getting the most out of every encounter with anyone you interact with—understanding the emotional needs of people for being recognized, appreciated, and rewarded. It's vital to building a solid organization, a winning team, and even a strong family. In fact, building strong relationships with your colleagues, team, or your network of contacts is a lot liking raising a family.

Another added bonus to acknowledging those kid-based emotional needs is that they give you the leeway to be hard on them when you need to be. It's a concept called tough love. Think about it—didn't you love your parents? But, at the same time, didn't you also fear them? And when I say fear, I'm not referring to intimidation; I'm talking about respect as well as fear of disappointing them or letting them down. Just like parents who give tough love to their children, you have to earn the ability to give tough love to your team or employees. It's a position that enables you to hold them accountable. This doesn't mean constantly pointing out their faults and flaws; it means using your relationship, which is built on respect and appreciation, as a means to ease the criticism. Once you've given them the approval and support they need, they'll be much more accepting and appreciative of your tough love. And because you've built a solid relationship already, that criticism will be much better received and much more effective.

Plus, when your team or employees' kid-needs are met, they're much more likely to go the extra mile because that recognition is a much more powerful motivator than money. As I mentioned earlier, it's easy to think and talk about money as a motivator but, if money is such a great motivator, then why don't more people have it? While the lack of money can be a disincentive, it isn't a long-term catalyst for performance. You give someone a raise or a financial incentive and they work harder for a day, or a week, or a month. Then, it's usually back to normal. That's because once they obtain whatever financial reward they're after, it won't continue to make them feel good. Study after study has shown that Americans are less happy today than their parents were in the 1950s, before the post-war economic boom created a large and prosperous middle class. People in the richest countries on earth are often less happy than those in poor, struggling nations.

Give people constant recognition and encouragement and they'll keep working harder for as long as their needs are being met. People are motivated by internal feelings and rewards far more than any external prize. They will go the extra mile and work harder for others than they will for themselves. Non-profit organizations, for example, have long depended upon the hard work of volunteers who are essentially working for no pay. These people often bring extensive skills to these organizations and dedicate long hours to a cause or a group. From a financial point of view, this makes little sense. But they're being richly rewarded in many other ways, one of which is being recognized for their hard work, often by the organization's leaders or the people they're helping. The kid inside is getting that attention he or she craves; his or her needs are being met.

Reaching those deep needs in people requires some effort. You have to understand the person you're dealing with and what motivates them, the same way a fisherman needs to know the kind of bait a particular fish likes to eat. For a manager, that task requires getting out of the office, knowing your staff and team, and giving them feedback on a regular basis. Do you need to praise a particular project they've been working on or the fact that they've been a loyal employee for the past five years? Praise must be sincere and it has to be linked to something tangible to be truly effective. Just saying "You're doing a good job," is not as effective as telling someone, "I like the way you handled that corporate account. Nobody has been able to make them happy until you started working with them." Or, if you're working with an individual in your organization who may not be the best producer but consistently gives a strong effort and is always doing what you ask, let them know you acknowledge and appreciate all that they do.

When I'm giving recognition to people, I want to make sure it's going to be as effective as possible for that particular person. I take my time to consider what will be the best course of action to empower them to ultimately be the best they can be. Now, some people might think, *Well, that's kind of calculating.* But if you understand my philosophy, which is as long as you act in the best interest of who you're dealing with, meaning you're doing the right thing, then you're right on target. In the end, it's all about positive results and this strategy will help you to get those. So, think your communication efforts through and come up with the best way to recognize an individual's effort so that they really benefit from it.

And there's a simple question you can ask yourself when you're trying to make sure those efforts will be on the mark: Do they address the needs of the other person's inner child? If you can answer "yes" to that question, you'll be ahead of so many others out there.

In a perfect world, we would all be well-adjusted, self-confident, well-assured, and self-secure. But what we must realize is that our childlike need for attention and acknowledgement is instinctive—we were born with it and it will stay with us as long as we're alive. I believe God wanted us to be givers and that's why he made receiving feel so good and giving feel even better. Sometimes life's complicated ways boil down to some very simple terms. We may all look like adults—and for the most part we act like adults—but don't ever forget what it's like to be a kid because deep down inside, we're all just kids, only bigger!

"CHILD DRIVE: Why is it as kids we are so relentless? We ask for the ice cream before dinner until we get it! We ask for a toy in the store until we get it! You want it? Then go back to being that kid who gets what they want because they never stop asking for it and expect to get it!**"**

Hmmm #6

Be an Asker, Not a Teller

When was the last time a day went by when people weren't trying to tell you something? **Hmmm** . . . never? I'm sure you've heard these famous words before, "Let me tell you something . . ." Tell, tell, tell! That's all people want to do. If they could just tell you about whatever great product they're selling or just tell you a little more about the business opportunity they're involved in or just tell you about their insights on the economy or just tell you how different their life would be if they didn't have all these problems or just tell you all the changes they would make if they were in charge . . . Wow, I'm doing it right now; I'm telling you all the things people are always trying to tell us.

Now, before we go any further, let me tell you (sound familiar?) that there's obviously a time, place, and a need for telling. So don't feel like you're already in the wrong if you find yourself telling people things. The idea of this **hmmm** is to realize the importance of the opposite of telling—asking—and how becoming an excellent asker will impact your ability to be a much better teller, which will ultimately help you be a much better achiever.

Questions are truly the lifeblood of your ability to gain knowledge. Whether you're doing the asking or being the one asked, a question generates a thought or a **hmmm**, as I like to say. Let me tell you (it's appropriate here!) about one of the greatest questions ever asked of me. As I sat across from a very wealthy man at dinner, he asked me this: "Did you know getting rich was easier than working for a living?"

At that particular time in my life, I couldn't even fathom that notion. Here I was struggling just to stay one payment ahead of the repo man, so as you might imagine, this seemed pretty hard to believe. All I kept thinking was, *This is easy for him to say.* But I finally got up the courage to ask him how that was possible. He responded with another question: "How many people do you know whose whole focus is getting rich every single day? Not just financially, but in every area of their life: spiritually, physically, mentally, emotionally, socially, and financially?" Obviously, I started to think about who in my life was like that, and honestly, although I wanted to give the man an answer, I couldn't think of any people I knew on that level.

While it had only been a few seconds, it felt like an hour passed. Eventually, he broke into my thoughts with his final question: "How many people do you know who are just getting by?" Now that was an easy one. "Everyone," I said. He then went on to provide me with one of the most important epiphanies (**hmmms**) I've ever had.

He said: "That's why getting rich is easier than working for a living. You have no competition. No one else is even trying." He continued: "If you want to get rich, it's pretty simple: look at what everyone else is doing and do the exact opposite." So there you have it. That's one of the reasons why I ask as many questions as I do because everyone else is telling.

Asking questions is an essential life skill. It's a critical element to building successful relationships. Ask, ask, ask, and ask some more. Think about it, when do you receive something? When you tell or when you ask? You got it, when you ask.

Have you ever gone into a car dealership where you already know basically what you want and the salesman comes up to you and immediately starts telling you how great this particular car is and telling you how great of a deal he could get you? You had made up your mind to buy the car when you walked in but the more this guy tells you about the car, the less you want it. Pretty soon, you walk away because he won't stop telling you about all the reasons why you should get this car. Now, suppose he had instead come up and began asking you about what you were looking for in a new car. Maybe he lets you tell him how you really like these leather seats and the navigational system and the gas mileage. Pretty soon, you've sold yourself and you're driving out with a new car, thinking, *Wow, that salesman was great!* And it's all because he just asked and let you tell.

What we all have to realize is people like to tell us things, particularly about themselves. That's why most people can't keep a secret because they have the itch to *tell* someone. Always remember that a secret is no longer a secret when the secret goes beyond the people that have something to keep secret. (Say that three times fast.) Be worried when you hear the obligatory, "Listen, I'm going to tell you something but you can't tell anyone else." Yeah right. That's as good as telling everyone else. Or have you ever been cornered at a party or, worse yet, seated next to someone on a plane who never stopped telling you about themselves? They go on and on and on, and you start to think about whether there is a parachute under your seat and if maybe you could pry open the cabin door and jump out.

On the other hand, when someone asks you about yourself, your interests, your children, your job, or just about anything that's important to you, your attitude is totally different. They're not a bore. No, now they're really interesting. And they're smart too! All because they asked and you had a chance to tell your story. We all love stories. From the time we were kids, we loved stories—from bedtime stories to family stories to success stories. We're the same as adults. We love to hear the stories of great leaders and inspirational people. Well, if we love to hear stories, it's not too hard to figure out we love to tell stories.

So with this point of reference, we have to be willing to let others do the story telling. Asking questions is the perfect way to begin a conversation—and a great way to keep it going.

Of course, it's okay to contribute to the conversation by telling things about yourself. But remember, if the purpose of the conversation is to establish a new relationship or enhance an already existing one, try to keep the spotlight on the other person. The key is to be genuinely interested, not strictly driven by your motives or desires to get what you want out of the conversation or relationship. Always think in terms of how you can help them versus how they can help you. Don't make your questions appear as though it is an interrogation and obviously don't ask questions designed to antagonize the other person. Keep in mind that you never know if the person you're talking to today will ever play a role in your success tomorrow. Stranger things have happened.

So get to know someone's goals, dreams, and aspirations. Get to know their family, their children, and their children's interests. What are their hobbies and things they like to do for fun? Find out what makes good days good and bad days bad. Bottom line: Ask, ask, ask!

In addition to the obvious benefits of building relationships, asking questions provides something else. It's the most effective way to get someone's attention and an excellent way to keep their attention. The reality is that we all carry an invisible TV remote with us at all times that allows us to change the channel in our heads on a moment-by-moment basis. Therefore, if we want to be effective at getting our message or point across, we must create enough stimulation to keep other people's channels tuned into us. The fact of the matter is our brains can only focus on one thing at time, meaning that in many instances you may think people are listening to you when in actuality they've already changed the channel.

Let me ask you this: Have you ever sat down with a friend and they wanted to get your thoughts on something and as they went on and on and on your mind drifted away (you changed the channel)? Maybe you were thinking about what you were going to have for dinner or maybe you were picturing your upcoming vacation. Well, during that brief departure, you literally heard nothing your friend said, so when they asked you the question, "So what do you think I should do?"—which is a question that requires you to refocus your attention back to your friend—you're at a loss for words because you weren't listening. Your response might be, "Whatever you think, I support you all the way." Not good. Hopefully you didn't just encourage your friend to give their bank account information to an e-mail scammer or to quit his job and play the lottery full-time in hopes of winning the jackpot.

My point of telling you this is because the same holds true for you. I'm sure there have been plenty of instances where people have been looking you dead in your face, maybe even smiling and nodding, yet they're either totally somewhere else, or worse, thinking to themselves, *I can't wait until this is over so I can get out of here.* To avoid being in that situation, simply ask questions. This will keep the other person engaged and the onus will be on them to stay involved in the conversation. If you ask the right questions, not only will you get and keep their attention but you'll also learn everything you need to know to make them happy. One of the simplest and most time-tested marketing adages is that if you help people get what they want, you'll get what you want.

I'm sure by now, you're saying to yourself, *Hmmm, this makes so much sense, so why haven't I been doing this all along?* Well, it's back to past programming again. Children begin as askers—who, what, where, why, and how. They never get tired of asking questions, and they never run out of questions to ask because they're curious about everything and they are open to learning. Did you know that the average four-year-old asks about four hundred questions a day? For parents with young children, that number might seem more like four thousand! However, those four hundred questions dwindle down to about twenty by the time the average person finishes college. Why the sudden drop off in being inquisitive? The combination of our formal education and our experiences in life convert us from askers and learners to knowers and tellers.

You see, there are two things that inhibit us from being askers. One is that we were led to believe that everything we learned and experienced has prepared us for success; therefore, why would we need to ask when *we know* (or so we think). The second reason is that so often we felt humiliated or inadequate because we may have asked a question that others may have perceived as stupid. Think about the number of times a classmate, peer, friend, family member, or even a teacher or parent have said, "That's a dumb question." Now that will make you want to ask questions, won't it? Once again, our past programming has limited our future progression. But that's why you're reading this book, to turn the page to a new way of thinking. Oh, and by the way, there is no such thing as a stupid question—only a stupid mistake. So, my philosophy is, it's better to ask a stupid question than make a stupid mistake.

Think about all the benefits of asking. It's how you learn, grow, and improve. An old Danish proverb says, "He who is afraid of asking is ashamed of learning." Every learning experience, every quest for new knowledge begins with asking. Think about how many better choices we could have made if we just asked. I believe that's the single biggest problem our country faces: we are uneducated in so many facets of life. What if we would have known to ask about how to live within our means, about how to avoid consumer debt, about how to build and maintain an excellent credit rating, and how to invest and save wisely? Many of the financial struggles we face today would likely be greatly reduced. What about asking how to have a successful marriage? Maybe if we knew that, the divorce rate wouldn't be over 50 percent.

There are so many questions we should and could have asked but we grew to believe that asking questions was a sign of weakness instead of a sign of strength. It's a mark of courage, while not asking a question is the mark of fear. Asking questions demonstrates your confidence. It shows people you don't think you know everything and it places you in a great light with others because they recognize your desire to get to know them. I assure you, people are not used to that. So as you incorporate this new concept of asking questions into your everyday life, watch the positive reaction you get from people and the amount of positive results you experience.

You probably have a question right now. Can these positive results you just mentioned help me make more money? Absolutely! As a matter of fact, your ability to ask questions will drastically improve your chances for increased financial success. Let's think about the role asking plays in business. First, think about two important concepts. Number one: money only comes from one source. Do you know what it is? Nope, not trees; nope, not banks; nope, not your parents, although that last one is partly right. That one source is other people. Period! That's why you have to be a master of people, and the best way to do that is to ask about them. Number two: as long as you create value equal to the amount of money you want, you'll get it every time. Of course, there has to be a need for the person you're dealing with, but it's all about showing value. And this is why asking questions is so paramount because you need to know what the value at hand is. Once you know the value then it's just a matter of exchanging it for the money. So the old, "Let me tell you about the features and benefits of my product or service!" or "Let me tell you why you should come on board with my company!" or "Let me tell you why I'm such a good person to work with!" won't work. What you have to realize is *telling* pushes information at you and *asking* pulls information from you.

Think in terms of fishing. How do you catch a fish? Do you push the fish away or pull the fish toward you? The answer is obvious, and by the way, *the value is the bait.*

So learn how to fish—ask questions. In some ways, your quality of life is going to reflect how well you ask questions. So using good questions in the right way is vital. There are two kinds of questions: open-ended questions and closed-ended questions.

Open-ended questions are used to gather information. Therefore, you're not looking for concise or one-word answers; you're looking for lots of information filled with specific details. You want to ask questions that are broad in scope and nature so you can obtain a broad range of information. Then you need to learn how to drill down with more specific questions to gain more and more specifics. Like this: "What is your number one goal right now?" The other person says: "I would like to be financially independent." Now you've set the broad parameters of the topic. Then you can begin to drill down into that answer to learn what that really means to this person and why. You might follow up with questions such as: "How much money do you feel you would need to consider yourself financially independent?" or "What types of things will you be doing with your money and your independence?" Let's say they would invest it and travel. Your next question would be, "Oh, really? What types of things would you invest in and where would you travel to?" Just keep drilling down for as much detailed information as possible. The initial questions paint the outline and then the follow-up questions fill in the details. Just be conscious of the questions you're asking because you don't want to come across as nosy or annoying.

As you already know from reading a previous **hmmm**, I'm a big proponent of practice, so here's a great exercise to become a better question asker. See if you can have quality and substantive conversations where you ask at least twenty questions. Of course, the idea is to ask good, logical questions that keep a conversation going but if you're truly interested in the life of the person you're talking to then you can start at the surface and then dig deeper and deeper. As they see your interest, they'll open up and tell you more. It won't be easy at first, and it will even feel a little uncomfortable, but if you stick with it, it'll become a mutually advantageous situation because you're getting what you want (more information), and they're getting what they want (your recognition of their importance).

Closed-ended questions are used in a manner related to getting affirmative responses. The goal of a closed-ended question is not to get a broad answer but to get "yes" responses to the questions being asked. An example of a closed-ended question using the same related topic as above would be, "So if I can show you a way to achieve the financial independence you're looking for, you'd be open to that, wouldn't you?" Or, "All of this hard work you're putting in so you can ultimately travel is going to make it worth it, isn't it?" At the end of each of these questions, all that is required is a one-word response. And because you're using information that is conducive to what this individual values, their responses are going to be affirmative. With the one-two punch of open- and closed-ended questions, you can not only gain the information you need but you can then take that information and create value in whatever it is you're trying to help that person obtain or achieve.

There are some of you who might be thinking, *Well, this sounds a little like manipulation to me!* It is if it's applied inappropriately. Unfortunately, that's commonly the case. Take martial arts for example. There are many skilled practitioners who carry the power to hurt others, but for the majority, the goal of their power is to protect and do good for others. That's my intent as well. My goal of sharing this with you is not so you can manipulate others but so you can persuade others—there is a big difference between the two. Let me explain.

Manipulation is a premeditated, devised plan in which someone goes to great lengths to induce or strong-arm a person to do something that fulfills the manipulator's wants or needs, regardless of whether it's in the best interest of the other person. The whole purpose of the manipulation is to give the advantage to the manipulator, not for the good and gain of the person being manipulated.

Persuasion, on the other hand, is the ability to open up and expand someone's mind to a new way of thinking. It's about helping them overcome their past programming and self-imposed limitations and enabling them to make a logical and educated choice that's in their best interest. Ultimately, true persuasion allows another person to comprehend what we are communicating, feel what we are feeling, and, as a result, become moved to do what we truly believe is in their best interest. To sum it up, I'll use a line right out of the *Spider-Man* movie: "With great power comes great responsibility." With this knowledge and skill, you now have great power—use it responsibly.

So what are we really talking about here? Simply, a basic human desire to be heard and understood. Everyone wants that, don't they? (Closed-ended question.)

Imagine it's Friday, the end of a long, hard week in which you gave it everything you got. To reward yourself, you decide to treat yourself to your favorite meal at your favorite restaurant. As you drive over, you're thinking about the thick juicy filet, the famous garlic mashed potatoes, and the sautéed string beans you're going to order and your mouth begins to water. Finally, you arrive, you get seated, and you say to the server, "I don't even need the menu—I've been waiting all day to come here. I'm ready to order. I'll have the filet, medium rare, with those garlic mashed potatoes you guys make. And please add the sautéed string beans."

The server takes down your order and leaves the table. You're waiting anxiously to get your food and you are so excited when it finally arrives. The server places the plate in front of you. As you look down, your eyes widen in disbelief. It's a plate of baked chicken, macaroni and cheese, and corn! Of course the first thing that runs through your mind is, *This is not my plate. This is not my wonderful steak!*

Then you call the server over and say, "Excuse me. I didn't order this. I ordered the steak, garlic mashed potatoes, and string beans."

And with a polite smile, the server replies, "Oh, I know that. But this is what I like."

At that point, to say you are flabbergasted would be an understatement. You might reply, "Have you lost your mind? You brought me what *you* like? What about what *I* want? What *I* ordered?"

I know this sounds crazy, but honestly, that's how most people communicate. That's how most people build relationships. I see it every day. It's not that hard; when someone wants a steak and you can bring it to them, don't you think they're going to be happier? Aren't they going to be more fulfilled? Isn't the transaction going to be a win-win? That person is getting the value they want and you in turn are getting the result you want.

So now is the time to take a look at your existing relationships, both business and personal, and ask yourself: *Do I know what they want? Am I giving them what they want?* If not, then start asking. And for those new relationships you're going to make, remember ask first and then tell. Finally, I hope this **hmmm** was a wakeup call for how things should be done because I believe there's a far greater authority than any of us who said, "Ask and ye shall receive." We all might want to heed that advice!

Hmmm #7

Everything Communicates

Most people probably think they know themselves extremely well. They think, *Hey, I'm a pretty cool person, fairly hardworking, successful, good to my friends and family, and just an all-around quality person.* But the reality is most people don't see themselves as they really are, and because they don't, they have no idea what kind of messages they are sending out into the world. Don't you think it's important to be totally aware of who you really are and, more importantly, directly in control of how others see you?

One of my favorite mantras is that everything communicates—including many things that are simply taken for granted and never even thought about. For instance, the greeting on your voice mail or lack thereof, the ancient food wrappers on the floor of your car, and your appearance, just to name a few. Whether you're aware of it or not, those elements are all sending out ongoing signals and messages about what kind of people we are. Are we trustworthy, responsible, and reliable? Would we be a good friend or business contact? Are we successful in business or in our career? People who don't even know us are picking up clues *about us all the time*—and that's why understanding that everything communicates is critical, because **success leaves clues!**

So, the first thing we must accept is that perception is reality, and this perception becomes the very thing that shapes the opinions of others about who we are. In other words, we don't live in a real world but merely a perceived world. You must ask yourself: "How do I want to be perceived?" I believe it is safe to say that all of us want to create a positive image of ourselves but often our good intentions are misinterpreted and could cause the wrong impression to end up in the forefront of someone's mind. That is why we must pay attention to all the little things (back to thinking three moves ahead) that can make the biggest difference when it comes to what someone else thinks of us. Whether they want to listen to what we have to say, whether they want to do business with us, or whether they want to be friends with us, the seemingly little things we do that send a message can play a huge role in our successes—or failures.

One of my absolute favorite and most powerful seminars, called "The Big Show," really accentuates this point. In this unique performance, a group of talented individuals come together, putting on dozens of different costumes, wearing numerous different hats, and playing many different roles and characters. From the Alien to the Baseball Player to the Lone Ranger to the Man in the Box, each scene delivers a specific message highlighting the theme of the seminar, "Life is Nothing but a Big Show."

Your life is no different. You wear many different hats, you put on many different costumes, and you play many different roles in your life. The people you communicate with are your fellow cast members and your audience. So how do you want people to review your performance? Because how you look and act in these various roles—in other words, the messages you're sending out—will strongly shape how people see you.

In this section, you're going to receive specific recommendations on a few simple but critical areas that directly impact the way people perceive you and interact with you—phone etiquette, business etiquette, image, and appearance.

The phone: A lifeline to good relationships

Have you ever really thought about how many hours per week we spend on the phone? If you're working toward financial freedom or looking to establish a sizable network of friends and colleagues, then, like me, you talk on the phone a ton! A good exercise I challenge you to do is to track the amount of hours you talk on the phone for a week, including all personal and business-related calls. Being aware of the amount of time you spend on the phone—and the important nature of some of those calls and messages we leave and receive—gives us a much greater appreciation for why we must be phone professionals. Isn't it safe to say that if we're going to do something that frequently and it plays such an important role, that we should do it extremely well?

The answer is obvious but most of the time the obvious is also the oblivious, meaning that these simple and common sense protocols are not applied. A quick tip for the wise—don't leave anything for assumption. I don't! In my twenty-plus years of studying and observing people, it has never ceased to amaze me how common sense is not so common. My goal throughout this book is to leave no stone unturned, to leave nothing to chance, to assume nothing.

Here are the ABCs of quality phonemanship. (I know some of you are thinking, *Phonemanship? That's not a word.* Well, you already know the answer—I don't care! And by the way, who decides what is a word anyway? If penmanship is a word, why not phonemanship? **Hmmm.** Is it not a word because it's not in the dictionary? The cool part about writing a book is that you get to choose the words. Phonemanship stays!).

Please set up your voice mail!

Let's start out with the perspective of you being the caller. It's probably not been too long since you called someone and a canned, monotone, robotic voice said, "You've reached 333-444-5555, please leave a message at the tone." And tell me, when that happened—especially when you're calling that person for the first time—were you not already forming opinions about that person? You might be thinking, "Is this even the right number? Do I really want to leave a message? Why doesn't this person have their voice mail set up?" In addition, the lack of a personalized greeting creates an impersonal, cold feeling. Is that the way you would like to begin a relationship? Remember, the quality of your life, your finances, and your personal fulfillment are directly related to and defined by the quality of your relationships; therefore, each and every action or inaction is going to play a valuable part in how these relationships evolve.

Also, consider this: Imagine your very inspirational and newsworthy story ended up across the desk of Oprah Winfrey and she was so intrigued by it that she instructed her staff to contact you because she wanted to meet you. But when they call you, there's no personal greeting, so because they're unsure whom they're actually calling, they decide not to leave a message. Whoa! Is this a missed opportunity or what? Now, of course it's possible that they would leave a message but my question for you is why would you even chance it? One of my favorite questions—as I mentioned earlier and one I would suggest you become a frequent user of—is to always ask yourself upon making a decision to do something or not to do something, what is the upside, and what is the downside? In this instance, isn't it clear that there is only a downside? While this may be an extreme example, the idea is for you to realize that every opportunity missed, regardless of how small or how big, will delay your arrival to the success you greatly desire.

Your personal greeting: positive or pathetic?

Okay, I know what those of you who have taken the time to record a personal greeting on your phone are thinking: "Whew! I'm ahead of the game on this one!" Not so fast! Have you actually listened to what your greeting sounds like? When people call you up, do they feel your energy and passion or do they feel your doom and gloom?

I'm sure we've all called people and were greeted by a weak, whiney, and depressed-sounding message. "Hi, this is Jim. Leave a message if you want and I'll try to get back to you." Jim might as well have said, "Hi, this is Jim, and my life stinks right now. I've got nothing going on so don't bother to leave a message because I'm contemplating throwing myself off a bridge." Now, I don't know about you but is this someone we want to spend much of our time talking to? Talking to this guy might cause us to have the same miserable outlook and make us want to throw ourselves off a bridge, too!

A great example of a creative, high-energy message is that of my good friend and fellow speaker and author, Les Brown. Wow, when you call Les and get his voice mail, it's like drinking five cups of coffee! Almost every day, Les takes the time to change his voice mail to include a different meaningful and thought-provoking message and he delivers it like he is standing before a crowd of thousands. Now, I'm not saying you need to do this—I don't—but this works for Les because it fits his personality, and that's his way of being unique—which, by the way, is something everyone needs to be. Remember, you were not born to fit in; you were born to stand out, so this a good **hmmm**. Find a way to be unique and a way to stand out—whether it's through a voice mail message or not—that makes you memorable and will help you create valuable personal and business relationships.

Anyone who's ever left me a message knows I make it a point to always have a very upbeat, positive greeting on my phone. The worst thing that can happen is people will think, "This Gregg Amerman guy has way too much energy!" I'll live with that. That's much better than somebody thinking, "Geez, this guy is a motivator, but wow, it sounds like his life is falling apart. Maybe I should reconsider listening to him or doing business with him."

So, *everything communicates*—including something as seemingly simple as a voice mail greeting. If you haven't already set up your voice mail, let me help you get it done. First, make sure your tone of voice is positive and upbeat. Here is an example of a simple and basic message. "Hi, you've reached the voice mail of (your name); I'm currently unavailable to talk with you personally; however, if you'll leave me your name, telephone number, a brief message, and a good time to call you back, I'll do my best to get back to you as soon as possible. Thanks for calling and have a great day!" Now you have no excuse—I've even given you exactly what to say! So, for those of you who don't have a personalized voice mail greeting or your message tends to be boring or low-energy, set it up now. That's right—stop reading and do it right now!

Lose the music

Let's talk about the decision to put a particular song on your voice mail or the phone for callers to listen to while it's ringing. Of course you can like whatever kind of music you want but isn't there a chance the person calling you might have a different taste in music than you do? And isn't there a chance they might be turned off by whatever song you choose?

Imagine this scenario. You apply for a management position and you feel good about the possibilities. Now, you're just waiting for a call from the company to set up an interview. However, when they call and get your voice mail it's playing a rap song and the person calling happens to hate rap. Ultimately, they hang up and decide to call someone else. You may have just missed an opportunity because of something petty. You have to decide now, what's more important, being right or being successful?

If you remember earlier in the book when I discussed having an I Don't Care attitude, which should mean you can have any type of music you want. But here's the key: You have to use this attitude in the right context. Having the I Don't Care attitude is supposed to help you succeed and attract people into your life, not help you fail and repel people out of your life. I don't care means standing for something you believe in that has merit and substance, and whether you put a probably meaningless song on your voice mail is not something to fight for. So why would you let thirty seconds of music send the wrong message for you? Once again, what's the upside versus the downside? You can listen to whatever you want on your own time but, when you're trying to present yourself as a professional, leave the songs on your iPod and off your phone.

The dangers of full mailboxes and unreturned calls

Okay, now we have our voice mail set up so we're ready for people to call us and leave us a message. Great! But . . . we can't receive a message because our voice mail is full. Not good! I'm sure you've been on the other end of this when you've called someone and couldn't leave a message because their mailbox was full. Doesn't that *just work on your nerves*? Don't you just shake your head and say to yourself, "How ridiculous! You mean to tell me you're so busy you can't even delete your messages?" Maybe you're even returning their phone call from earlier in the day but now you can't even get in touch because they couldn't be bothered to delete a few messages! What type of perception is this creating about this person? Understandably, if you're in a coma or worse, dead, well then, you're excused. But I don't think that's the case for the majority of the people who allow this to happen. Some people might say, "Well, Gregg, I was out of the country." Great, how about just changing your voice mail to: "I will be unavailable for the next week or so; please try me back on (your return date) or you can e-mail me and when I return I'll get back to you." Wouldn't that be a much better option that would take just seconds? Most importantly, what kind of perception would it create?

Callers would have nothing but appreciation for the courtesy of letting them know about your unavailability. Only upside!

If that doesn't sink in, consider this: What if Publishers Clearing House Sweepstakes was calling to inform you that you just won a million dollars! But, because they couldn't leave a simple voice mail, your prize goes to some other lucky person! How angry would you be at yourself? I hope you've got it: NO FULL VOICE MAIL BOXES!

Now let's consider something else that happens to most of us on a regular basis: unreturned phone calls. We leave a message with someone and they never call us back. So what is our perception here? We probably think one of the following:

1. They must be really busy.
2. Maybe I'm not important enough to call back.
3. Do they have an issue with me?
4. They obviously don't want to talk to me.

There are many other possibilities as well. The fact is, not returning a phone call is irritating and unprofessional. If someone doesn't want to talk to you, wouldn't you prefer they call you and say, "Please don't call me anymore?" At least that's some type of closure rather than it seeming like they vanished or they were abducted. Once again, this is a terrible perception to create for yourself. The scary part is this is not just a dysfunction of individuals but even of billion-dollar companies. Think of the many companies we deal with that provide lousy customer service and don't even return our phone calls. If we want to get anything done, we must keep persisting. This is another golden opportunity for you to set yourself apart from the masses and build a strong, trustworthy, reliable reputation, while most don't. And with great ease, I might add. Simply return phone calls, even when you don't want to, even if it's just to say, "Don't call me anymore."

The headset horror

Now, let's move on to another thing most people are oblivious to: the old wireless earpiece. It's like this little piece of plastic is stuck permanently in their ear. It's incredibly annoying to others, yet the people who wear them all the time have no clue. I personally surveyed two-hundred-fifty people who were asked the question, "How do you feel when you are talking or eating with someone who is wearing a wireless earpiece?" Ninety-two percent—yes, 92 percent!—found it annoying, obnoxious, and rude. When asked if they actually told the earpiece-wearing person their feelings, less than ten percent had.

By the way, I also answered the questions, too, and I was one of the 92 percent and one of the less than 10 percent who spoke up. I've sat across the table from the phone-earpiece wearers at restaurants. I've been in meetings with them. I've even done seminars where some of the people in the audience were wearing one. It drives me crazy. I recall one of my personal coaching clients was wearing a telephone earpiece during one of our coaching sessions. When we met later for dinner, he still had it on. It was at that time that I encouraged him to remove it and explained why. He did and, to this day, he only wears his earpiece at appropriate times. You see, when you have that earpiece in, it makes people feel like you're not giving them your undivided attention and they feel like at any moment you'll be distracted by a call. It makes you seem impersonal and it can also make you appear unapproachable because people can't tell if you're on the phone. It can also make you seem like you think you're some kind of big shot, that you're so important you need to be available to answer your phone at *all times.*

If this sounds familiar, you might be thinking, "But I can't miss a call!" Well, what about all the potential business you're missing from all the people who don't want to be around you or, at the very least, wonder about your sanity because of your addiction to a wireless headset? I guarantee you they're out there. Wouldn't it be a shame to lose a business opportunity, or a new client, job, sale, or friend because of that? It just makes people feel uncomfortable. So if you're not driving your car, by yourself at your desk, or working for the CIA— *take it off.* When it's an appropriate time to talk on the phone, feel free to use it, but when it's time to socialize or interact, remove it. Again, *everything communicates.* Don't let a little piece of plastic in your ear communicate the wrong message or create the wrong impression for you.

Okay, let's go over some additional dos and don'ts when it comes to phone interaction:

1. *Don't raise your voice.* How many times have you heard people talking so loudly on their phone that not only can you hear their entire conversation but so can people in the next time zone? It's annoying, unnecessary, and it's not the kind of attention you want. Learn to have an inside voice, please.

2. *Stop taking calls during movies, meals, and meetings.* Wow, how rude is that? Put your phone on silent or vibrate and put it away and leave it there unless the call is urgent. Most of us have lived without cell phones for most of our lives so you can do without it for a few hours. It shows respect and that's a great thing to be known for. Oh, and one more thing, put your phone away when it's quiet time with the family. Somehow, I don't think Alexander Graham Bell had the notion that his incredible creation would take precious time away from the family when he invented it.

3. *Don't be a text message junkie.* Listen, I do my fair share of text messaging. But I assure you, during a meal with someone, while I'm playing with my kids, or during a meeting, I don't stop every few seconds to text. I'm sure that, like me, you've been in the company of someone who, instead of focusing on you, spent most of their time looking down at their phone pecking away at the keys. It's amazing—I've seen friends and even married couples go to dinner and, the whole time, both of them are texting others. What's the point of going out when you're

not going to spend quality time with that person anyway? People text while they eat, while they're having conversations, while they work, even while they drive—none are good. Once again, there is a time and place; make sure it's the right time and the right place.

4. *When making or receiving a call, put a smile on your face.* People can sense your energy right through the phone. When you smile, they'll hear it in your voice. Everyone prefers to deal with a happy person rather than the alternative.

5. *When making initial contact with someone via telephone, start the conversation by asking, "Is now a good time to talk?"* Some other simple questions you can ask are, "Do you have a few minutes?" or "Are you available to talk right now?" This serves two purposes: one, you'll gain instantaneous respect for being cordial and for valuing their time, and two, you'll ensure that you have the undivided attention of the person with whom you're talking. Think about how many times you're in the middle of doing something or on the other line and someone calls and immediately begins rambling only to have us interrupt them to say, "Listen, I have someone on the other line" or "Now is not a good time, can I call you back?" Think about the times we've done this to others. All of this could have easily been avoided with just the simple courteous habit of asking, "Is now a good time?"

6. *Leave short but detailed phone messages.* People appreciate knowing what the call was in reference to and, in many cases, this can save the person with whom you are trying to communicate a significant amount of time. This could allow them to be prepared when they return your call. Also, make it a habit to always leave the number you would like to be called back on with your message. Remember, don't make assumptions. They may not have your phone number available to them.

7. *When talking on the phone, shut off your TV or at least mute it.* If not, you're likely not an attentive listener or, even worse, the other person might think you are distracted, that you watch a lot of TV, or even that you're a lazy couch potato. Remember, *everything communicates*, and something as simple as the TV on in the background can create the wrong perception. People who call me probably think I never watch TV because I either turn it off or it goes to mute. So I'm giving away one of my secrets: I always want to control the perception I'm creating for myself and simply eliminating background noise allows me to give my undivided listening attention and there are no other perceptions that can be formed. For those of you who work from home, this is especially important: create the perception that you are busy working and taking care of business.

8. *Master conference call etiquette.* In today's world, lots of business takes place via conference calls and there are definitely guidelines to follow. It is always best when entering a conference call to be in a location that allows you to be focused on the call—somewhere quiet with no background noise. Background noise is anything you can hear because whatever you can hear, *every other person* on the call can hear as well. I know some of you are thinking, "Come on, Gregg, don't you think I know this?" Well, to be honest with you, most people don't! I've been on thousands of calls where I hear kids screaming, dogs barking, music blasting, TVs playing, dishes being washed, cooking, driving, and other people having a conversation. It's rude, terribly unprofessional, and completely unnecessary, but unfortunately most people don't pay attention to the details so these things continually happen. Making sure you're not one of these individuals will allow you to interact openly without disrupting the call. However, if you are in a situation where this is not possible, then always place your phone on mute. In most cases, you will be directed by the conference call moderator or host on how to place your phone on listen only. But with technology the way it is, I'm sure your phone has a mute button. Find it! Finally, make sure you always have a pen and paper available to take any pertinent notes (quietly, of course!).

The bottom line is: keep in mind you are constantly working on your identity and how you are perceived. So if you're guilty of any of these—and you know who you are!—get to work on fixing them *immediately*. These are ways of building positive relationships one action at a time. When you think about all of this, the phone is just a tool we use to make communication easier, to make relationships easier, and to make life easier, so never forget that *everything communicates*; in the process, you just might make the late Mr. Graham Bell proud, too.

The basics of business etiquette

Sending the right messages out via your phone is only part of the challenge in helping others perceive you favorably. So let's move on to how everything communicates in a business setting.

Master the handshake

This goes without saying but one of the first things people will remember after meeting you in person is your handshake—especially if it's a bad one. It's always amazing to me how some people pay so little attention to something so important. I'm sure you've met someone for the first time and stuck out your hand, only to have that person crush your fingers with their grip. At that moment, did you think to yourself, *Oh wow! I'm so excited to meet this person!* Or did you think, *What an aggressive jerk.* (Or something more colorful but this is a G-rated book!) Or how about when you come across the opposite—what some people call "The Dead Fish"? You grab a limp, lifeless mass of flesh that seems to have no bones or muscle inside, like a wet noodle. It makes me cringe just thinking about it!

In both cases, these handshake styles create an immediate impression. With the first, it's a person with a big ego who feels a need to be dominant, in control, and aggressively tries to overpower you. With the second, it's a person who lacks confidence and has low self-esteem and low energy. Both are *BAD!* A good handshake should fall somewhere in the middle—firm without being too forceful. The impressions we want to make are trustworthy, honest, confident, and personable. It should make someone want to know more about us.

People do judge a book by its cover

Beyond your handshake, what else about us sends a message? How we look, of course! You know the saying "Don't judge a book by its cover?" Great in theory but let's be realistic. People do judge by appearances; therefore, we must act accordingly. We're all walking, talking judgment machines and we are constantly evaluating all aspects of a person, including, and especially, appearance. It's one of the quickest ways people form their opinions about us, before we've even said a word. And this is true of everything. Why do you think restaurants put so much money into the presentation of the food on the plate? Why do companies spend so much on commercial packaging? It's all about how they want their product to be perceived because people care about how things look. It's called marketing! And just like a product needs to be presented well to thrive in the market place, so do we.

Now, it's not my goal to be your personal fashion consultant here, but I do want you to start paying attention to and recognizing what's appropriate in a business setting. Are you going to an interview, to lunch, or to the beach? Think about the type of setting you'll be in and dress accordingly. What someone wears to an interview for a job as a sound technician with a rock band is going to look very different from what someone wears to an interview for the sales director position at a marketing firm. And when you're not sure, it's always a good idea to err on the side of more professional instead of more casual.

Whenever I have a speaking engagement, I always inquire about my audience and the objectives of the presentation so that my dress attire will be conducive to the audience and the message. Obviously, if I'm playing the role of one of the many Big Show characters, that's one thing. But there are times where I'm speaking to kids so I may dress in jeans. If it's a corporate function, I may wear a suit, including cuff links, a watch, and polished leather shoes. There are a broad range of presentations and instances, and you must adjust accordingly. Your clothing and accessories can send a strong message: they express success and confidence and can really help you immediately identify and establish acceptance from your audience. On the flip side, dressing inappropriately can be a tremendous detriment to whatever it is you are trying to accomplish.

If you ever find yourself unsure as to how you should dress, always overdress rather than underdress. Is there a chance that someone will be turned off by my suit and tie? Possibly, but not likely. But would there be people who'd be turned off—or wouldn't take me as seriously or even listen to me in the first place—if I chose to wear a T-shirt, shorts, and flip-flops and walked in unshaven? Absolutely.

In the same way, any time you see Donald Trump, he's wearing a business suit, a tuxedo, or golf clothes while he's on the links. That's because the image he's trying to project all the time is one of power, wealth, and success. (Now, you may not like his comb-over hairstyle but it's all part of his image, his brand, who he is. So it works for him.)

It's all about looking the part. Think about it: how comfortable would you be boarding a plane and seeing the pilot with a pair of jeans and a T-shirt and long hair? Probably not very. Why? Because we've become accustomed to a certain image of a pilot. That shaggy-looking pilot may be able to fly that plane as well as any but we wouldn't believe it based merely upon the pilot's appearance.

How influential can dressing appropriate be? Well, if you saw the movie *Catch Me If You Can*, starring Leonardo DiCaprio as the true-life role of legendary con artist Frank Abagnale, the possibilities are endless. DiCaprio's character dressed up as a pilot and literally had people believing he was a pilot. Abagnale was able to cash $2.5 million in fake checks between the ages of sixteen and twenty-one largely because he was able to make people believe he was an airline pilot, as well as an attorney, a college professor, and a pediatrician. It's not because he actually had skills in those fields. It's because he was able to look the part.

You can bet Abagnale knew that *everything communicates*—especially your personal appearance. Now, obviously the point of sharing this example is not so you can manipulate people or to make yourself out to be something you're not, but to simply show you how important your appearance is to how people perceive you and receive you.

Keep your car clean

What about how your car looks? Of course, I'm sure most people would love to drive the finest automobiles made in order to send the message that they're at the top of their game. Which is fine—there's nothing wrong with wanting a nice car. But what I'm talking about is not so much about the model or the price tag but the car's *appearance*. What do you think about the owner when you see a car coated in so much dust that someone has written "WASH ME!" on it with their finger? And what about the inside? Have you ever had to wait with your hand on the door handle while the driver throws all the empty cans and plastic bottles, food wrappers, and papers into the back, just so you can have a place to sit?

You can bet a messy car is sending a pretty strong message to anyone who sits in it—or even sees it. Think about this: What if, unexpectedly, you were asked to join a very important lunch meeting with some important business clients and you were asked to drive? Would you make the most of the opportunity by sending a strong message with a nice, clean car? Or would you be dying of embarrassment and preparing tons of excuses to explain why your car was such a mess?

Now, I'm not saying you have to have a car so clean you could eat off the floor mats or have a shine so bright you can see your reflection in it because, believe me, I know what it's like to have kids, and kids and a clean vehicle don't even belong in the same sentence. I'm just saying that if you'll be driving around with clients or taking your boss to lunch or anything else that involves your vehicle, make sure it presents the image you want it to. Because—I'm sure by now you know what's coming here—*everything communicates.*

Who should pick up the tab?

Many times our business dealings take place over lunch, dinner, or drinks as socializing is often times a big part of our business relationships. And at some point, you'll face the dilemma of who pays.

Well, that's not an easy question to answer, because it all depends on the situation. Sometimes, the person who requested the meeting will pick up the tab. Sometimes, the person who wants something from the other—the chance to present a business opportunity or idea or maybe advice about something—will pay. Sometimes, you just agree to split it.

But in all of these situations, make sure you use good manners and set an example of being a class act. Here are some simple ways to handle the tab. First of all, never feel that you are required to pick up the tab, unless of course you committed in advance to doing so. Don't feel obligated to pick up the tab even if the person you're having the meal with doesn't offer to pay anything. Just pick up the check and simply say, "Let's just split it." Now, if the amount of their portion of the bill is far greater than yours, simply say, "Here is my share, with tax and tip." If someone else is picking up the tab, it is always a respectful gesture to at least offer to pay your portion of the bill. You don't have to insist because some people get a great deal of pleasure out of treating. Some instances may call for you to insist on paying your own way or picking up the tab yourself. You'll know when that is the right thing to do.

Of course, if you're the one being treated, *always* thank the other person both for the meal and for their time—and do it twice. It's just good manners and it will leave a lasting impression of what an appreciative person you are. While this may seem like such an obvious thing to do, you'd be amazed at how many people don't do it!

While I can share numerous stories with you about this type of behavior, one instance stands clear above the rest. I had lunch once with a business contact. We both had much to gain from this relationship, so there wasn't a clearly defined right or wrong way the tab should be handled but I was prepared and felt good about picking up the tab. We had a nice lunch and everything seemed to be going well—until the check came. I placed my card down to pay and there was no response. Not an offer to pay, not an offer to leave the tip, not even a thank you, nothing. My contact just sat back in their chair and waited for me to take care of it. Even worse, at the conclusion of our time together, when we were standing there saying good-bye— giving them a perfect opportunity to acknowledge that I picked up the tab—they didn't even thank me! I couldn't believe it. And at that moment, the relationship was over for me. I immediately lost respect for them both as a business connection and even as a person. You can tell a great deal about someone in situations like that. They made a lasting impression and not in a good way.

So here's a little etiquette to remember. If someone picks up the tab, immediately say thank you. Upon saying good-bye for the final time, say, "Thanks again for the meal." And finally, if you really want to leave a positive impression, send a quick thank you note, text, or e-mail, telling them how much you appreciate them.

So, whether it's a meal, tickets to an event, a round of golf, or anything else for that matter, have manners, be gracious, and be classy when it comes to treating or being treated. Why? Because everything communicates!

Image is everything . . . well, almost everything

What people experience when they call you on the phone, how you dress for an important meeting and everything else we've talked about in this **hmmm**, it all relates to a much bigger picture—it's about creating a positive image for ourselves. I know you've heard the phrase, "Image is everything." Well, it may not be *everything* because you're not going to make millions of dollars just because you dress sharply and have good phone manners. But it sure does make up a significant piece to the puzzle.

Here is a perfect example of how the wrong image could unknowingly cost you a fortune on many levels. I want to preface my telling of this true-life coaching experience and how this changed an individual's life by stating that I have never judged a person by the color of their skin, the length of their hair, their size, or anything else. I judge a person by their character. Remember, I was a foster care social worker in the heart of New York City so I've had to work with all types and none of it ever changed my outlook.

However, I am like most people when it comes to certain expectations about how things are supposed to look and through my vast experiences I have come to learn what works and what doesn't. I am also brutally, but tactfully, honest. I want people to tell me the truth about things I could potentially improve or change and that is the only way I know how to be. In the early to mid-1990s, when I was working in Atlanta in a sales and marketing capacity, there was a guy I worked with who was very skilled, smart, personable, and was doing well for himself. But, there was one thing I felt was holding him back from really excelling: a big gold tooth front and center in his mouth, gleaming at people every time he smiled. Now, I want to reiterate, it did not bother me. This was a guy I hung out with on a regular basis but I believed his gold tooth was affecting his business and income. You see, as I said earlier, we are all in marketing. Whether it's a product or a person, the first thing people are going to look at is the packaging. For instance, if you're an athlete or a music star, then having a gold tooth might add value to what you're doing. But if you are a businessman trying to relate to a broad audience, it's not going to do you any favors. Once again, you can take the attitude that this isn't right or fair but it's not always about what's right or fair; it's about what works. And in thinking this way, a lot of times it works out in your favor.

So one day, I pulled my colleague aside and asked him a very simple question: "If there was a way you could possibly increase your production, would you be open to hearing the possibilities of how?" He said, "Of course I would! How?" I then asked him if it was possible to remove the gold tooth without it being a major issue. He told me he could, and I said that if he did that I believed he would see a huge impact. I told him, "If it doesn't do what I think it will, you could always put it back in. So it's worth a shot, isn't it?" He agreed, and he took the gold tooth out.

Sure enough, several months later, his income had increased substantially and he had achieved one of the top positions in the company. I was so happy for him and, of course, it made me feel great that something I encouraged him to do worked out so well.

Now, does this make me a genius or clairvoyant? Of course not—it's just marketing. Look at business magazines or any type of business media, what do you see? Mostly clean-cut, well-groomed, professionally dressed people. Just like you wouldn't feel comfortable going to a KISS rock concert and having them take the stage in suits and short-styled haircuts, you probably wouldn't feel comfortable if your potential financial advisor showed up for the first time wearing sweatpants, a tank top, a Mohawk haircut, and tattoos on both arms. Even if this advisor had a great track record, in most cases people would never believe it anyway. You have to come to the realization that you can't expect the world to revolve around you and your beliefs; therefore, you need to make adjustments along the way to get the results you're looking for.

Mirror, mirror

Most people can make major improvements to their image by paying attention to these four little words: look in the mirror. Then ask yourself if the person looking back at you is sending the image you want to send to the world. But just to make sure you are looking for the right things, here's a checklist.

1. *Check for stray food in your teeth after a meal.* There is nothing worse after eating a salad than having a piece of lettuce covering one of your teeth, making you look like you had one of your teeth knocked out. The scary part is most people you

talk to won't even tell you it's there. That's why you have to check for yourself.

2. *Keep a pack of breath mints in your car, desk, pocket, or purse.* People won't remember you if you have good breath but you'll be the highlight of everyone's jokes if you kill them with your bad breath.

3. *Trim or eliminate all the hair that makes people say, "Look at that hair!"* You know what I'm talking about: nose and ear for men, mustaches and chin hairs for ladies. Men, shave well enough so you don't have stray patches of hair or nicks all over your face or neckline. Ladies, there's an amazing array of bleaching and waxing products out there.

4. *Iron your clothes.* Of course your clothes will get wrinkled throughout the day. But don't leave the house and start your day wrinkled.

5. *Invest in good footwear, both casual and dress.* People always notice shoes. (Oh, and get them shined once in a while.)

6. *Keep your fingernails clean.* Even if you're a mechanic, clean them when you're done working. Ladies, make sure your nail polish isn't chipped—or don't wear polish at all. Nothing is worse than some nail polish on, some off. That is not a style that I'm aware of.

7. *Wear deodorant, and a little cologne or perfume doesn't hurt, either.* People love things that smell good.

While there are many more things we can add to this list, hopefully this is a good start in helping you pay much closer attention to the details involved in making a good impression. Everything I've covered in this **hmmm** all boils down to this question: how do you want to be perceived by others? It's more than just wanting to be liked; people's perceptions of you have an impact on your income, your success, and your happiness. They can determine whether you make a sale, get a new client or prospect, get the job you want, meet the right person, or catch a lucky break. Or they can keep you from getting all of those. And when that happens, the worst part is you might never know what you lost because people won't tell you that they didn't like the music on your voice mail. Or they never called you again after your mailbox was full the first time. Or that your greeting was depressing. Or because your car wasn't clean. Or you had extra-long nose hairs Tarzan could swing on. Or you just didn't convey the right image. You often can't quantify what your loss was. Keep in mind one lost deal could be a thousand lost deals.

Unfortunately, most people won't be as honest as me. They won't tell you the things you need to improve or to clean up, so my advice to you is if you want help, ask for it. I ask for help all the time. If after a meal there's no mirror around, I'll ask someone to give me the okay for food in my teeth. I have no problem asking people with fashion expertise about the latest styles of clothing so I can have the best appearance possible. I'm fortunate because my wife loves to shop and knows the current fashions so I can't take credit for my wardrobe. But believe me, it feels good to know when you are presenting yourself well; you exude more confidence and are more comfortable interacting with people.

The bottom line is to think about the image that you want to project to the world and be conscientious of what you're actually projecting. Many times, there's a considerable difference between those and we're not even aware of it until we step back and look at ourselves with a very critical eye. Get outside of yourself so that you can see yourself as others see you. Then, be proactive in making sure you're always sending the right message.

So, one last time (well, at least for right now): *everything communicates.* And it's up to you to do everything you can to make sure everything you're communicating is as good as it can be because you are what you communicate.

Hmmm #8

Fear, Doubt, Pride, Ego:
Are You a Prisoner in Your Own Mind?

Have you ever thought about the magnitude of being confined to a prison cell for the rest of your life, sitting on death row waiting for your death sentence? Some of you may be thinking, *Where is he going with this hmmm? This is a pretty grim beginning.* But it's certainly not as grim as the reality that many people in our society spend each and every day in a kind of solitary confinement. Now, the solitary confinement I'm talking about may not have a physical presence, such as cinderblock walls of a cell, steel bars that keep you locked in, the ball and chain attached to your leg that keeps you from going too far, or shackles around your wrists that keep you from doing too much. No, it's far worse; it's a prison we built for ourselves, a metaphoric structure we created with the help of four partners in crime: Fear, Doubt, Pride, and Ego.

Each of these plays a big role in derailing us from achieving our dreams. In fact, if you take a look at every failure, shortcoming, or unfulfilled dream in your life, each of them is guaranteed to have at least one of these four inhibitors attached to it. So many of us have cowered to this Fear, succumbed to this Doubt, surrendered to this Pride, and yielded to this Ego. These self-imposed limitations cause us to exist rather than live, to waste all of our gifts, purpose, and talent, and to ultimately make us prisoners in our own minds.

Maybe you've been so focused on finding security for so long you now have what you weren't even looking for: maximum security. An imprisoned life is not one that anybody should live, because when that happens, you commit the most serious crime of all—murder. What do you kill? Your dreams. And when your dreams are dead, what else is there to live for? So, let's work together to break free, to escape this prison and live life to the fullest.

First, let us understand that these four criminals and weaknesses of Fear, Doubt, Pride, and Ego are really heroes and strengths that have just gone astray. Let me explain. I believe each of us is a superhero armed with great natural power; however, as with most things, not knowing how to harness those powers can easily turn them into weaknesses—or even worse, into dangers. It's my goal to help you gain control of your superpowers and turn these menaces into powerful allies.

Fear (the cinderblock, or the first superpower)

Fear is actually a biologically conditioned response, a feeling and an instinct we were all born with. Each of us has the sense as to when something is not safe or something is not right, and that creates that "fight or flight" response. I'm sure you've had a few experiences in your life when, knowingly or unknowingly, fear took over and caused you to act in response to an unexpected situation. This is nothing new; it's the same response that helped primitive man fight off saber-toothed tigers and other attackers. The effects of this response include an accelerated heartbeat, dilated pupils, faster breathing, and increased speed and strength.

Saber-toothed tigers might not be around anymore but that biological response is still ingrained in each of us. Think about the hundreds of men and woman who were endangered or lost their lives thrusting themselves into the burning and crumbling Twin Tower buildings during the devastation of 9/11. Or the brave people on that same day who committed to taking down the fourth plane before it could reach its final destination. Or the young college students at Virginia Tech who moved to action by holding the classroom door shut while gunshots were fired randomly at innocent people. These individuals turned their fear into a superpower, making it their strength.

However, we can also think about instances where people who were in life-threatening, frightening, or downright dangerous situations said, "I was so scared I couldn't move!" They were paralyzed by fear and fell prey to this weakness. Now, of course, the real culprit is not this type of fear, because grand dramatic events are the rare occasions. I'm talking about the day-to-day threat, the fear that we battle every day: fear of failure, fear of success, fear of inadequacy, fear of losing, fear of what others say and think, fear of being judged, fear of being wrong, fear of the economy, fear of death, fear of being alone. Wow! That's a lot of fear running around. So what do we do in the face of all this fear? Unfortunately, most of us usually do nothing.

We allow that treacherous criminal to kill our spirit, because when we fear not having money, we stay in jobs we hate. When we fear the idea of upsetting our significant other by speaking our mind, we put up with garbage that makes us miserable. When we fear failing, we don't even try. We're paralyzed by fear, so we do nothing, and by doing nothing, you *are* in fact doing something—you're cementing some more of those heavy cinderblocks into the cell walls.

Hmmm.

So how do you conquer your fears instead of letting them confine you to this cell forever? Well, consider this study from the National Aeronautics and Space Administration (NASA). Researchers were curious about why some pilots and astronauts completed their missions without suffering motion and stress sickness while others consistently suffered from those ailments. After researching, NASA found that only *one factor* distinguished the two groups. Those without physical problems had acknowledged in advance that they were going to be afraid. So the defining lesson learned from this study was that those who admitted they were scared were able to gain control over their fear versus the ones who wouldn't acknowledge they were afraid. When you can admit beforehand that you're scared—even if only to yourself—you have turned your weakness into your strength.

Microsoft founder and billionaire Bill Gates has said on numerous occasions, "I have a fear of failure. Absolutely. Every day that I come in this office, I ask myself: *Are we still working hard? Is someone getting ahead of us?*" I probably don't need to tell you the track record of Microsoft and Bill Gates but I will anyway . . . Microsoft is one of the most successful companies in history and Gates is a man who constantly makes the "world's richest" lists. Gates' admission of his fear illustrates my point: feel the fear, embrace the fear, and do it anyway. Use fear to fuel you, not stifle you, and before you know it, you'll pulverize those cinderblocks into nothing more than dust!

Doubt (the bars, or the second superpower)

We have to defeat this evil nemesis known as doubt with the most powerful superpower of all . . . "Zero Doubt." How you handle doubt will definitely play a major role in whether you reach your goals and fulfill your dreams.

Doubt and fear are dangerous partners. Left to rule on their own, they're the perfect pessimistic pair. They keep you trapped, quiet, and insecure. They keep you unmoving. And they hold you stationary, keeping you from experiencing life.

But, just like fear, doubt kept in check is a strength and a superpower. A healthy amount of doubt means you're doing your due diligence first. It forces you to consider potential obstacles and diversions beforehand allowing you to plan in advance how you'll handle them instead of being swallowed whole midstream. It makes you analyze, strategize, and question things before you do them. It gives you a chance to do your homework. It demands that you consider the downside and the risks, which helps you become more realistic and more prepared for what it will take to achieve your goals and dreams. It allows you to be a little less emotional about the mere possibilities.

I like to consider myself an optimistic realist, which means I expect the best and plan for the worst. I don't listen to what people say. I watch what they do. As you'll read in **Hmmm #11**, my two favorite words are "we'll see;" therefore, when the green of the cash hits the white of the table, the deal is done! Another benefit of doubt is it reminds you to cross all the *t*s and dot all the *i*s, meaning get a signed contract before you do the work, read the fine print, and confront all of your concerns. If you go into everything with blind faith, you'll undoubtedly be blindsided, and a healthy dose of doubt is the perfect preventative measure for that.

But the key word there is *healthy*. Doubt starts to spiral into the unhealthy category when it overtakes you completely. When it shuts down creativity and replaces it with stagnancy. When it kills your hopes and destroys your dreams before you even give them a chance. *If you doubt everything, you don't believe in anything.* If you're that kind of person, you're probably too busy doubting everything to notice the steel bars that are your only view of the outside world.

Hmmm.

Start planning your escape by not allowing doubts to flourish in your mind. Start asking "why?" instead of "why not?" Replace "can't" with "can," substitute "try" with "do," and use doubt as a tool to make you sharper, allowing you to cut through those steel bars like butter!

Pride (the ball and chain, or the third superpower)

Our pride is at the core of our psyche. It can be viewed in several different ways: as a sense of one's own self-worth; the state of being proud; or excessive self-esteem. Theologians and scholars often cite pride, the most serious of the seven cardinal sins, to be the root of all other evils. That's pretty serious stuff, isn't it?

Well-known author Dale Carnegie once said, "When dealing with people, let us remember we are not dealing with creatures of logic. We are dealing with creatures of emotion, creatures bustling with prejudices and motivated by pride and vanity." I couldn't agree more. I've always said that people use logic as a way to justify their decisions and actions, but behind it all stands the real decision maker: emotion, which is mostly made up of pride.

But, just like there are good and bad versions of fear and doubt, there are good and bad versions of pride. If you think about it, the difference between having the ball and chain of pride or the superpower of pride is reflected in the way we use it. If you take pride in something—like your family and how you raise your kids, your job, career or business, your work ethic, how you give your time and money to charitable organizations and the community, the relationships you have with your family, friends, and business associates and colleagues—then that's pride at its best. That's pride-power (I know, another made up word).

In addition, we all want a sense of pride when we are acknowledged for the good work we do. We all want to feel a sense of belonging and enjoy moments when others we respect note our accomplishments. From childhood and beyond, we will always want a strong self-esteem, strong sense of self, and solid sense of security, and often times much of that development comes from the many proud moments we all hope to be a part of. From when our parents, teachers, family members, peers, and other respected people told us they were proud of us, to later in life, when we are proud of others we have helped to shape and influence, to when others say they are proud to know us. All of this helps the superpower of pride to fuel us to work harder, achieve more, and be better because that type of pride creates passion for who we are and what we do.

On the flip side, however, pride has sort of an evil twin. Think about the phrases "He needs to swallow his pride" or "Her pride got in the way." In other words, instead of us "taking pride" or "having pride," we can have too much pride—and we all know too much of something can be very dangerous. Pride becomes useless pride when we take an unyielding position that we are right, that we know what's best, that we don't need help or need to listen to this person or that person. We ask ourselves, *Why should I have to change or make adjustments?* It's that very pride that will keep the ball and chain anchored around your leg, preventing you from moving forward successfully.

Think about this—if we believe our way is the only way but our results aren't nearly what we want them to be, couldn't that mindset be a self-imposed limitation? Your pride has officially made you a captive—it has locked you up in your circumstances. Your pride is making you hold onto your past programming and beliefs. It's preventing you from learning new ideas, philosophies, and techniques. It's keeping you from asking for help because you believe it's a sign of weakness, of being unsuccessful, of feeling inferior and inadequate, or that you may actually be struggling and you wouldn't dare put yourself in a position to be exposed as not having it all together all the time.

So now we're faced with a serious dilemma: the choice between being real or being a fraud—between being honest with ourselves and others or continuing to hide behind our false sense of pride. I say, come clean. People will have more respect and will hold you in higher regard and will be prouder to know you because you are real and you are strong enough to ask for help. That you have the pride to know that all great individuals have had their fair share of trials and tribulations, failures, disappointments, and moments of needing help. I know it's true for me. While I've certainly enjoyed many proud accomplishments in my life, including the financial success of having the big house and nice cars, I've also experienced the failures—including foreclosure and bankruptcy—and I can honestly say that I'm proud of it all. Not that I'm suggesting this was my goal or should be a goal for you. But the challenging times helped me realize what really matters and what I'm most proud of: my awesome family and the many great people in my life who are proud to know me, not because of what I have or whom I'm perceived to be, but for who I really am and the substance and character I am made of. I am proud to know I have weaknesses; I am proud to know I don't know everything; I am proud to know that I have so much to learn and grow; and I am proud to know I will always ask for help and support when I need it. I hope this is the kind of pride you want, the kind that's self-assured about being proud of yourself.

Because the alternative is not pretty. It's pride running the show, keeping up a constant front of successes, material possessions, college degrees, and money. It limits the ability to grow, learn, and interact. The focus and worry is so honed in on what others think that when the time comes—and it will—that help and support is needed in some way, maybe financial help or advice or just a shoulder to cry on, it will never come, because it will never be asked for. And there it is, the ball and chain that you created and that you keep adding to, link after link, every day.

Hmmm. Does this sound familiar?

By contrast, someone who's not held prisoner by pride isn't above asking for help. They value themselves enough to know that their well-being, success, and happiness is worth way more than possibly appearing weak, needy, or less of a human being to others. They don't let their pride get in the way of anything; instead, they get their way by controlling their pride.

Unlock this ball and chain of pride by focusing on what's really important—who you are as a person. If you want to be free, put a lid on your false pride, the kind that comes from possessions and perceptions. Having pride in yourself doesn't have to do with money or what people think of you. You should be proud because you're a good person, a good friend, good to your family, a hard worker, or just because you do the right thing (hopefully, you're all of these things!). In other words, when it comes to the right kind of pride, it's all about the content of your character.

Remember, there is a fine line between the ball and chain and the superpower of pride. As an old English writer, Charles Caleb Colton, says, "To know a man, observe how he wins his object, rather than how he loses it; for when we fail, our pride supports us; when we succeed, it betrays us." **Hmmm.** Don't forget those words!

Ego (the shackles, or the fourth superpower)

The ego is probably the hardest of the four criminals to fend off because, as Austrian psychiatrist Sigmund Freud explained, the ego is a complicated beast. The ego is a critical self-organizing principle of the human personality. It's kind of like the command center of the psyche that coordinates the different aspects of the self. Without it, Freud asserted, we could not function.

Think about that. The ego is the command center and has a hand in every move and action one takes; therefore, the challenge is much greater than just functioning—it's about unlocking the shackles that keep most people dysfunctional. When you think about conversations in regards to the word *ego*, they're not usually very positive ones. You don't hear people saying things like, "He had such an exciting ego" or "Thank goodness for her ego, that really made the difference." No, it's more like "What a jerk, do you think his ego could be any bigger?," or "Her ego is so huge, it makes me sick," or "They're an egomaniac." So to say dealing with a person like this is unpleasant is an understatement. The majority of times we have to deal with someone like this, it's a complete turnoff, very de-motivating, and overall just a miserable experience.

We all know or know of individuals who have lost control of their egos and lost touch with reality. They're the dictators, control freaks, and power mongers, people who use intimidation and fear as a way to rule and motivate. They spend time tearing you down in order to build themselves up. Then you have the people who constantly look in the mirror admiring themselves, the people who take credit for all of their successes and lay blame on others when they have failures. These individuals believe if it's not their idea, it can't be a good one, or they pooh-pooh an idea at first and then later claim it as their own. They constantly manipulate and have a need to control everything and everyone, and the scary part is they believe it's in the best interest of everyone. At the same time, they never ask or listen to anyone—so how would they know anyway? These are the people who regularly boast and spout off about how great they are, how much money they make, all the scholastic accomplishments they've achieved, the amount of square footage of their house, the type of cars they drive, and a laundry list of all the other things they have and all the other things they've done.

But, strange as it might sound, these people are so busy trying to get you to think highly of them that they usually don't think too highly of themselves. And as a result, they're imprisoned without even knowing it. And because they don't see themselves as they really are, they overcompensate, thereby shackling their very existence to be someone they're not. Imagine having such a deep void of self-confidence and lacking so much positive self-image that any and all the great people you've attracted into your life now appear as a threat to your success. Sad, isn't it?

Well, I've witnessed it. During many of my speaking engagements and advanced training programs, I constantly give credit where credit is due. I'm not a big believer in the notion that someone is "self-made." I mean, come on. Did we birth ourselves? Did we change our own diapers, feed ourselves, and teach ourselves? Of course not. Regardless of the level of success any individual might have achieved, there were at least a couple of influential people who contributed to that success. No one is self-made—*homemade*, yes, but not self-made. I tell you this because this self-made attitude can happen to anyone. Don't think, *Not me*; think, *Is that me?*

Here are a few hints that this could be you:

- If you catch people rolling their eyes ten seconds after you open your mouth.

- If you're talking to someone on the phone and the only words they're contributing to the conversation are "uh huh."

- If you're in meeting after meeting and everyone sitting around the table smiles and nods affirmatively without ever talking or giving feedback.

- If you're walking down the hall and people duck into cubicles that aren't even theirs just to avoid you.

The reality is no one would want to work for someone like that or be on that person's team or be friends with them or be married to them, so why would you want to be them?

Now, these are the serious cases of ego. But don't think you're out of the woods just yet—as I mentioned earlier, our egos are the most dangerous criminal of all, and they can affect us even in the most subtle ways. There are many whose egos trap them. They're too busy putting on false airs to everyone around them to take a hard look in the mirror. They buy things they can't afford, just so they can say, "Look what I have! Look who I am!" The worst part: they don't even realize it. In fact, egos are a big part of the reason for the recent real estate crisis and debt accumulation: because people weren't honest enough with themselves to admit they couldn't really afford that massive new home and everything else they purchased on credit.

As a result of their egos, *so many* people sit in their self-constructed jail cells—imprisoned with financial uncertainty, unhappiness in relationships, dissatisfied in their careers—sometimes for years, maybe even for life.

Hmmm. Is there a way out?

Fortunately, an unhealthy ego is not necessarily a life sentence or a death sentence. You can learn to control and use your ego as the superpower it was designed for and, as a result, you'll be free to achieve the successes and dreams you're capable of. The first thing is to understand that having a healthy ego means being confident, not cocky. A healthy ego means you're honest with yourself and genuine to everyone around you. A healthy ego is knowing that money talks and wealth whispers. A healthy ego allows you to play for the team first and to be the best on the team second. A healthy ego enables you to focus on positive results instead of focusing on being right. A healthy ego keeps you competitive, aggressive, and productive, but at the same time compassionate, appreciative, and caring. A healthy ego means having humility—knowing that you're a part of the world instead of believing it revolves around you. So keep a close watch on your ego, and if you feel yourself slipping, make sure you reread these last few pages to remind you of who you don't want to be.

When it comes to the four villains of Fear, Doubt, Pride, and Ego, there's a fine line between letting them lock you up or set you free. It all boils down to you controlling them—instead of letting them control you. Fear, Doubt, Pride, and Ego can be your greatest assets or your biggest liabilities. They can help you to achieve, be fulfilled, make money, be confident, feel good about yourself, and lead a life that you're proud of and happy with. Or they can confine you, keeping you struggling financially, fearful, pessimistic, weak, and feeling bad about yourself and your life.

The best part is the key is in your hands. It's your choice. Lock yourself in a prison in your own mind, or unlock your true potential to a life of financial freedom, success, and personal fulfillment? Only you hold the key!

Hmmm #9

The Four Core Principles of Leadership

Are you ready to step up and lead? Because one thing I know is that we need more leaders. It's evident that our country is at a critical juncture in its history. The economy has gone through one of its toughest stretches ever, jobs are less secure than ever before, homeowners are struggling to pay their mortgages, real estate values have declined, people are concerned about how they'll pay their bills, and retirees are watching their money for the future dwindle. In addition, if this wasn't enough, millions of people are worried about how they'll pay for health care as the population's overall health continues to deteriorate. And let's not forget about the rampant incidents of unnecessary and senseless violence, criminal activity, and unethical behavior.

Everywhere, people are looking for answers and hope, but all they're getting is disappointment and frustration as it seems that no one is leading the way. Why is it that we rely on CEOs who make the big bucks, politicians whom we have no personal relationship with, governmental agencies, and corporate giants to lead us? We don't even know if we can trust these individuals and institutions, let alone let them lead us. For all we know, they could be a significant factor in why these things are happening. But honestly, we can't place the blame on them. True leaders don't place blame; they actually take responsibility and look to find or create their own solutions. That's what today's world commands and desperately needs—a group of new doers, leaders, thinkers, and innovators! So, are you ready to step up and meet the challenge—and lead?

Think about some of the US presidents throughout history, such as George Washington, Franklin Roosevelt, Abraham Lincoln, and John Kennedy just to name a few, considered excellent leaders or British Prime Minister Winston Churchill still revered for his leadership. The same is true for Henry Ford, Thomas Edison, and Andrew Carnegie—business icons whose inventions and wisdom helped lead America into a new era of innovation and prosperity. Mother Teresa, Mahatma Gandhi, Nelson Mandela, and Martin Luther King Jr. are all synonymous with great leadership that had nothing to do with money but with helping people with their unimaginable struggles in life. These are just a handful of the countless leaders who have impacted our lives and who have made drastic changes and brought hope, pride, financial growth, newfound freedoms, and the chance to live a superior quality of life.

So notwithstanding or minimizing the importance of the past, and taking nothing away from the great work done by these iconic men and women, we are faced with the needs of the present and the rapidly approaching future. I know that many people believe that the president should fix the problems the nation faces as well as the world's problems but it will take much more than one person to address these uncertain times. And while we should all try to be as supportive as possible of our president regardless of how we voted, each of us must recognize the importance of leading ourselves.

Think beyond politics—take Microsoft founder Bill Gates, for example. Gates is certainly well recognized for his leadership and for the impact his company has made during the computer and technology era we live in. He's among the wealthiest people in the world, but even he, with all his great wisdom, lost billions in 2008. Obviously, I think we would all like to be in a position to lose that kind of cash. But the point is that it's time to stop looking to everyone else for leadership and start looking within ourselves. That doesn't mean we shouldn't have mentors, coaches, advisors, and leaders in our lives. It just means we need to take the responsibility of educating and developing ourselves to be one of those leaders.

So, unless you've been living in a cave, you've probably heard of Lincoln, Mother Teresa, Churchill, King, Gates, and the others I mentioned. They're all leaders who are recognizable on a global scale. Though leaders of their caliber and quality may seem rare, especially today, that's even more the reason why everyone should work toward developing their own leadership skills to improve their lives, personally and professionally. Once again, I cannot stress the importance of how our world certainly needs you more than ever before to step up and lead.

You see, all leaders—whether they're the captain of a sports team, the student body president, the manager of a team of people, or President of the United States—embody unique qualities that make people want to follow them. Think about it. You've met people in your own life who've inspired you and made you want to be a part of their team, their business, their campaign, or their crusade. In fact, US President Dwight Eisenhower, another great American leader, described leadership as "The art of getting someone else to do something you want done because he wants to do it." In other words, leadership involves motivating people to do what is in their best interest, which, in my mind, is why it is so important for people to strive to be strong leaders for themselves and for others.

If you're reading this book, it's evident you're not looking to sit back and just follow someone else. Yes, you understand the importance of being a good follower for the purpose of being a good leader but you want to be out in front, leading others. I'm sure some of you are already leaders, and I bet many of you already know you're naturally inclined to becoming leaders. But there are probably others of you who, although you envision yourself a leader and have the desire to be one in some way, aren't quite sure what that really means and how to go about achieving it. Well, you've come to the right **Hmmm.** As legendary football coach Vince Lombardi famously said, "Leaders aren't born, they are made. And they are made just like anything else, through hard work."

So, let's get started forging you into the leader we all need you to be.

Over the years, thousands of people have come to my seminars, and I have to chuckle when I think about the number of times I have said to the audience, "I'll give anyone a hundred-dollar bill if you can tell me the four key leadership principles."

Pretty soon people are yelling out all kinds of leadership characteristics. "Passion!" "Vision!" "Enthusiasm!" "Integrity!" "Honesty!" "Hard work!" "Positive attitude!" "Leading by example!" Just trait after trait. Word after word. Description after description. Sometimes, somebody will get one of them but most of the time they never get to the foundation of real leadership. You see, it's not just about qualities, characteristics, and traits; it's about philosophy, values, and a way of life. At least this is what my experiences, both successes and failures, have taught me. Since you're reading my book, I'll trust that you're going to be open to these four key leadership principles, or at the very least give them a good **hmmm!** Understand, it's not that the answers the individuals at the seminars yelled out are wrong; they're just not applied in the right context. But once you've finished this **Hmmm,** you'll have a clear understanding of what I'm talking about.

The reason I came up with these four principles is that true leaders (by this I mean someone who's ethical, honest, and does the right thing) are almost always synonymous with success. Sure, you can be a successful follower. But, like it is with a dogsled team, the view is always best for the lead dog.

Over the course of my career, I believe I've come into contact with close to a million people, whether it was through one-on-one interactions, speaking to small groups, or addressing 10,000 at a time. All those interactions have made me fairly astute about the critical aspects that make up a leader. And over the years, I've also realized that the people who were leaders in some facet of their lives shared similar philosophies. It didn't matter what field they were leaders in or in what area of their life. Their leadership styles weren't really the essence; it was more the common bonds of these four key components. And these individuals had them whether they knew it or not.

Of course, there are many different qualities found in leaders. Some are excellent public speakers. They can motivate their followers with words. Others are very competent in their field; their expertise puts them ahead of the pack. However, to be a true leader, I believe it all comes down to the following four core principles.

1. *Listen to the voice of God.*
    Now, before you react and think this is going to be a religious sermon, I assure you, it isn't. So relax and be open to what I'm sharing. This is neither about religion nor

whether you attend church or temple or pray every day. I'll leave that to your individual preference. Instead, think about this—great leaders are from all types of religious backgrounds and some may not consistently discuss religion or go to a physical place of worship. But most will tell you they believe in God in some form or fashion.

Let me explain. Inside of each and every one of us, we have this spiritual voice. Some people think of it as a sixth sense that taps into a different realm of knowledge beyond the five senses of touch, taste, smell, hearing, and sight. This sixth sense is that intuitive voice within all of us. Some people call it a gut instinct or just a feeling, but if you listen to that voice—to your inner spirit—it will provide you with the direction, guidance, and often the answers to questions that aren't obvious in the day-to-day physical world we all live in. This is a form of spirituality—what I call listening to the voice of God.

We all have this ability. But few of us actually listen to it—and that's the key. You must listen to that voice and tune into it, because it's coming from a higher place and a greater power, and it manifests itself within you. It's the voice of faith. The voice tells you to move forward when everyone else is confused and doubting. If you learn to listen to that voice, it will tell you exactly what to do at the right time and in the right situation. It will give you the knowing to press ahead to victory.

Now, I know right about now some of you are rolling your eyes and asking yourselves, "What is he talking about? I'm supposed to be hearing voices? Am I supposed to be Joan of Arc?" No. I'm talking about the voice of faith, your spiritual voice, your higher self, or—as I call it—the voice of God. Call it what you want. It doesn't speak with words, but it speaks with clarity when you're listening. Often it starts as a feeling, but as you listen more closely, it soon becomes a knowing of what is right and what is wrong. It's there inside of you, but it's not your own thoughts and feelings; it's much stronger.

I can tell you that listening to this voice is not always easy. Sometimes the voice won't make sense to you; it may tell you something that doesn't seem logical. You may listen and then think to yourself, *That's crazy.* Why? Because it's easier to listen to ourselves since we're the ones physically going through these situations. We might have our money invested in something we are doing well in, and the voice says, *Get out,* but we don't because of greed. What happens? We lose our money. Or we jeopardize a relationship because of lust or selfishness, when the voice tells us, *Don't even put yourself in that position.* This is one of the hardest things you'll ever have to do but it's paramount to your ability to lead.

I once worked with a very successful, fast-growing company where I earned a considerable amount of money. I spent many years working diligently to build my business and income to great heights, and then that voice came one day and said, crystal clear, *Leave it all behind.* So, I did. Although it made my situation immediately more difficult, I can tell you that it was one of the best decisions of my life. I can also tell you that there have been other times when I didn't listen, and it cost me dearly. I can say that the small percentage of the time in my life that I didn't listen to that voice, or I listened to it and ignored what it was trying to tell me, proved painful. In fact, I'd say the hardest lessons I've learned in life have happened because I didn't listen when I should have. Conversely, when I did listen, even though I didn't necessarily understand it, and it may not have even made sense at the time, listening always turned out to my benefit.

Our logical minds might tell us we should see it before we believe it, but if you want to tap into a higher sense of clarity and wisdom, you have to believe it before you will see it. That's what faith is all about. That's what your spiritual guide, if you allow it, brings to you. But you have to have the patience to listen. The answer may not always come exactly when you want it, but it will always come. And know that one day it will make sense, or at least provide comfort and closure to a particular situation. So, start listening, because there is no better advisor than God himself.

2. *Control your thoughts and emotions.*

This is a critical one—mainly because of the repercussions if you don't! It's simple: either control your thoughts and emotions or they will control you. In essence, you are either the master of your mind or a slave to it.

Let's break down just how important it is to control your thoughts and emotions. Life is an accumulation of decisions, isn't it? And all of these choices we're making and all of these decisions we're moving forward with are ultimately going to affect the rest of our lives. Therefore, to the best of our ability, we must be able to control our emotions so that our thoughts will be clear and sensible when making that choice or decision. You see, the majority of people *make* their choices and decisions on emotion and then *justify* those decisions with logic and reasoning.

For instance, if you're purchasing a new home, you obviously will consider many factors: location, schools in the area, construction of the home, and of course the cost. But at the end of the day, for most people the final decision will come down to how they feel about living in this home. Because if it doesn't feel right, then you won't be happy, and that will cause another emotional decision—moving to a different home. Of course, that wouldn't be logical, but remember, the point is people don't make logical decisions; they make emotional decisions.

Let's look at another great example—marriage. Now, this for the most part is not logical unless you are doing it for tax purposes, trying to become a citizen in this country, or just seeking companionship in your elderly years. But I'm talking about marriage in the majority of cases. Do we have some kind of checklist to fill out and do we conduct interviews with a number of potential spouses? Do we ask: Can you cook? Do you work out at the gym? How much money do you earn? What is your credit score? Now, I'm not saying you wouldn't want to learn about your prospective partner and that you wouldn't be curious about all of these things, but that wouldn't be the basis of your relationship. It would be about how you feel about this person. Are you attracted to them? Do they make you feel warm and fuzzy, if you know what I mean?

Mastering control of your thoughts and emotions is paramount because your emotions are going to play a role in what your thoughts are—which are then going to impact your choices and decisions. One of the best examples I can think of is from my own life—and I'm sure many of you will be able to relate to it. When I first started out in my own business career, most people were negative and unsupportive. Many told me I was crazy. If I didn't control my emotions—thereby allowing these people to influence me—you might not be reading this book right now. (**Hmmm!**) But because I controlled my emotions, it allowed my thoughts to say, *Hey, these people might care about me and may even have good intentions, but they don't have the experience, expertise, or qualifications to offer me advice. So I can't listen.* As a result, I stayed focused and on track, which paved the way for my success.

Another time, I reached the point as one of the top people in the company I mentioned earlier. Unfortunately, even though most people would assume this was a great place to be and an incredible opportunity, it was quite the contrary. I was miserable. Although it went totally against the logic of earning a lot of money and being financially stable, I resigned from that company and left behind my income, many friends, and even some family members.

That's the power of emotion. Yes, your thoughts, logic, and reasoning are essential. They form how you make a plan and determine the right approach. But your emotions are your fuel—your power to carry it all out. They work hand-in-hand and you have to control them, or they will have you and your life out of control!

Picture yourself as a soldier in the military, if you're not already one (and if you are, thank you so much for all that you do to provide and protect our freedoms). Think about being on the front line somewhere with a mission that involves extreme risk and potential loss of your life. Logically, there is no way you move forward, but because a great soldier has control over their thoughts and emotions, not only can they move forward, but they can do it coolly and calmly. Amazing, isn't it? So controlling your emotions allows for better thoughts, which will lead to better actions, which of course leads to better results and will determine, on a bigger scale, the course of your life. Leaders recognize that their ability to lead really boils down to something as simple as managing their thoughts and emotions, because everything else stems from them.

Leaders cultivate their ability to respond, not react, which is another crucial part of being a great leader. We were all given instinctive emotions, such as fear, anger, lust, sadness, happiness, and excitement. And it's important to realize that all of us have the right to have whatever feelings and emotions we want to have. But also know that if we want to be great leaders, we need to use that right responsibly so we can benefit and enrich the lives of ourselves and those around us.

In this way, controlling your thoughts and emotions doesn't mean you ignore them. It means you recognize them and act on them appropriately, not randomly and uncontrollably. You choose the right time and the right place to express your emotions.

Take, for example, something almost everyone can relate to, a rather common situation that often triggers some immediate intense emotions (if you let it). Let's say you're on your way to an important appointment or to the airport to catch a flight. You got a late start, so you're already anxious because of how close you're cutting it, and you're cruising along well above the speed limit when out of nowhere the highway becomes an instant parking lot. In the snap of a finger, stress, anxiety, and—worse—anger completely take over. You're literally sitting there overwhelmed with frustration—and you explode! Before you know it, you're cursing up a storm, and your blood pressure is skyrocketing. You're thinking, *What the *&^% is causing this? Who the *&^% is causing this?* You could easily jump out of your car and look for someone to yell at for making you late. **Hmmm!** Sound familiar?

Listen, I hate traffic as much as the next person, and living in Atlanta and travelling to cities like New York and Los Angeles, I deal with my fair share of it. But sitting in traffic presents everyone with an easy opportunity to control his or her thoughts and emotions. Why? Because you can't do anything about it, so why make it worse by letting your frustration and anger get the best of you? Of course, if cursing, yelling, and engaging in all-out road rage would enable your car to sprout wings and launch itself above the traffic, then by all means, I'd be the first to do it. But until somebody finds a way to make that happen, what's the point? You're moving no faster, getting to your appointment or the airport no sooner . . . period. So you might as well remain cool, calm, and collected and save your frustration and anger for something worthwhile. In this case, you would simply call to delay your appointment or reschedule your flight. You just have to recognize that sometimes in life, "It is . . . what it is." Understand that all emotions have purposes; it's just a matter of being in control of how to use them. You see, in this instance, anger was useless, but at other times it can serve a purpose when it's used to move someone to action. We've all seen this from a parent, teacher, or coach when they were angry and may have even yelled at us, and we moved to action. I've used this method of motivating over the course of my career. Some of those times, I wasn't even angry; it was just a way to get something done.

Controlling your thoughts and emotions also applies to how we respond or react to people. Consider this story, which made the rounds through the restaurant industry a few years ago. During a busy lunch shift at a popular restaurant, a server was in charge of taking care of a table full of attorneys. This was her only table for the day, so she wanted to treat them like gold to ensure she got a great tip. She made sure their glasses were always filled, their food arrived on time, and they had everything they possibly needed for an enjoyable meal with their colleagues. After several hours and several bottles of wine, the bill ended up well over $500, and after thanking the attorneys as they left the restaurant, the server went to clear the table and to see what kind of a tip they left her. What she saw astonished her: a $5 bill lying on the table.

The server snapped. She grabbed the bill and ran into the parking lot before the attorneys could leave and started screaming at them. "How dare you basically stiff me after the stellar service I gave you! You can just keep your $5—I don't want it!" she yelled, throwing the bill on the ground. One of the customers paused, looked at her in amazement, picked up the money off the ground, and then walked back into the restaurant, coming out a minute later with the $100 bill they'd left on the other end of the table. "I guess you don't want this, either, then," he said, before getting into his car and driving off.

Wow. Can you imagine how terrible that server felt because she'd not been able to control her thoughts and emotions? That she didn't even allow the possibility of there being a perfectly good reason for the $5. Maybe there was a good reason, like someone added an additional tip to the nice one the attorneys had already left. Couldn't she have handled the situation far differently by controlling her thoughts and emotions and simply asking the attorneys, politely, why she had only received $5? Was there a problem with her service to warrant such a low tip? I'm sure the response from the customer would have been, "Oh, you must not have seen the $100 we left for you. You did a great job." Instead, she lost $105 and probably her job.

Controlling your thoughts and emotions is vital because it is one of the few things in life you can really control. That's the thing about life: You may not always be able to control your circumstances, whether the traffic moves slow or fast, how people behave, or what cards you're dealt, but you can always choose how you think and feel and how you choose to react to all of those things. So control your thoughts and emotions, because that's how you control your life—and what makes you a truly effective leader.

3. *Express gratitude.*

A great leader understands the importance of having trust, respect, and loyalty from the people they are leading, and expressing sincere and genuine gratitude creates that type of relationship. Now, that should not be your motive for doing it, but by default if you don't express gratitude, you express ingratitude. First, let's distinguish between being grateful and expressing gratitude. As William Arthur Ward, an American scholar, once said, "Feeling gratitude and not expressing it is like wrapping a present and not giving it."

We all know people who we would consider ungrateful. But if you were to sit down with that individual and were to tell them point-blank that you thought they were ungrateful, I'd bet they'd deny it and even give you a long list of things they're grateful for. In reality, in almost all instances people are grateful, but their lack of expressing that gratitude creates a perception that they're ungrateful.

So how important is the expression of gratitude? Well, it's the difference between having close and distant friends, and the difference between the people you'll work with and for and the ones you would never work with or for. It's the difference between the good words people will speak about you or the poor ones. It will determine the quantity and quality of the relationships you will have for life.

All true leaders express gratitude to those around them: to colleagues, coworkers, and business partners, to friends, to supporters, even to family members. In a work environment, the people who work for or with a true leader know they appreciate the good work they do because leaders let them know. They express their appreciation in a clear and tangible way. They praise in public. They take their staff out to lunch, write handwritten notes thanking employees and members of their team for their hard work, and give their people the afternoon off sometimes "just because." These things don't take a lot of time, money, or effort to do. But the payoff they have is extraordinary. As the Chinese proverb says: "If you want one year's prosperity, grow grain. If you want ten years' prosperity, grow trees. If you want 100 years' prosperity, grow people." Think of gratitude as the fertilizer in that process.

Just saying thank you or I appreciate you, are easy, efficient ways to express gratitude, but it's amazing how many people don't do it! I can't tell you how many people

I have spent countless hours on, coaching, helping, supporting them without even the glimpse of appreciation. I'll never understand that. Don't be one of those people. Somebody picks up the tab for a meal—remember to say how much you appreciate them. A colleague helps you prepare an important presentation or does a presentation for you—remember to say thank you. Make it a habit to say thank you or I appreciate you for even the smallest thing, and you'll be making gratitude a subconscious habit, one everyone should have.

Keep in mind that expressing gratitude, even in seemingly small ways, lets others know you're grateful. Expressing gratitude not only makes the recipient feel good, especially if they see you as a role model and someone they respect, but it will also make you feel good as well. Furthermore, who wants to have a relationship with someone who's ungrateful? Enough said!

Finally, please don't forget that at some point in your life, someone was leading you, helping you, or supporting you. Remember to express how grateful you are for those who played an important role in your success.

4. *Be consistent.*

Right now, you might still be wondering: *How can passion, determination, honor, work ethic, or integrity not be key leadership principles?* I agree with you that these qualities are keys to being a leader. But without the word "consistently" in front of each one of them, they are just words.

What's the point of being passionate if you are not going to be *consistently* passionate? What's the point of having integrity if you don't have integrity *consistently*? What's the point of being focused if you are not going to be *consistently* focused? What's the point of being an optimist if you are not going to *consistently* be optimistic? What's the point of having a strong work ethic if you're not going to have a *consistently* strong work ethic? You see, anyone can have these qualities on a temporary basis, but that won't make them a leader. Unfortunately, most people are most consistent at being inconsistent.

Here's a prime example of the concept and results—or lack thereof—in relation to consistency. Think about the countless people who want to be in great physical shape and want to look really good. So they join a gym, with all the good intentions of getting up every morning and getting a good workout in. However, the majority of the time it plays out something like this: You go for three days the first week and miss the following week because you got busy. Then the next week you go for two days then miss six days, and then you go for four days straight, but then miss a month because of travel and other obligations. Then you go three days and miss two weeks; then you go for two days and miss a week. Do you realize that if you did that for an entire year, although you would have gone to the gym quite a few days, because you didn't do it consistently, you would see no noticeable change? However, if you had gone to the gym three days a week for the entire year, you would see a vast improvement in your health, your fitness, and your body.

It's the same way in every area of your life. Consistency serves dual benefits. One is this: your consistency will pay off in terms of your personal results. Every successful person and great leader put forth a consistent effort that ultimately produced a result. The second reason that consistency is so powerful is because it's the absolute one thing you can control with respect to what others see—and will most certainly judge you by. This means that even when you are doing something or building something and there may not be any tangible results to see, people will notice your consistency, and that will give you respect and credibility. And as a leader, respect and credibility are essential to leading people, organizations, families, and companies. Without consistency, it's common for someone to dismiss another person's new project, endeavor, goal, or dream as a fad or a phase they're going through.

Think about this: consistency eliminates that doubt and makes people curious. And the more consistent you are the more confidence people tend to have in you, and the better chance they will follow you.

Martin Luther King Jr. is probably one of the greatest examples of consistency. From the first day he uttered the words "I have a dream," the phrase became his mantra and, eventually, one of the most revered quotes in history. Regardless of all the death threats, doubters, skeptics, and naysayers—some even from his own camp—and the backward thinkers of that time, King stood strong and consistent. He didn't say, "I have a dream" one day, and the next day say, "What was I saying, this is a nightmare." If that were true, none of us would even know who he was. But of course, we all know the reality.

So a leader isn't a here today and gone tomorrow kind of person or a one-way one day and another way the next. You don't treat your employees or organization wonderfully one day and then behave like a dictator the next. You don't set a lofty goal one day and subsequently change it every day thereafter. You become successful because you consistently achieve smaller goals every day until you hit your lofty goal.

Even in the face of failure, a leader is consistent. When ordinary people fail at something, they often take that as a sign that they should be doing something else. Or they give up completely on ever achieving that goal or desire. But successful people look at failure as a chance to learn and grow, a way to figure out where they went wrong and how they can improve upon it. In fact, in their study of the "working wealthy," *The Middle Class Millionaire* authors Russ Alan Prince and Lewis Schiff found that when confronted with a bad outcome, nearly 77 percent of millionaire executives "tried again in the same field." That's because they're leaders—they were consistent in their efforts to keep going.

Consistency also helps to shape your identity, good or bad, and it's how others come to know you. People are always going to be judging us, and consistency is one surefire way to secure the reputation we want for ourselves. It's kind of like your calling card. Take the fable of the boy who cried wolf, who because of his consistent lying made people not believe in him, which really hurt when the wolf really was there and he needed help. Consistency is about doing what you say you're going to do; then people believe you're going to follow through, and you build up a high level of confidence that people have in you. It's a powerful combination—consistency and confidence.

So if you add consistency to the other key ingredients of leadership, then you've really prepared something special, something that's going to bring you financial independence, success, and personal fulfillment. You're going to be a true leader, and others will see it in you. They will see it because you're trusting and listening to the voice of God, your inner voice. They'll know your temperament is rock solid because you control your thoughts and emotions and respond, not react, to challenges and circumstances. They'll feel your gratitude and appreciate it, because they'll feel your love, which is why you'll be loved by others. But most importantly, they'll see all of this consistently—which is why they will follow you. And that's what these times need, more strong leaders for people to follow!

So as you finish this **Hmmm**, don't just say to yourself, *Well, that was good reading.* Don't just walk away with a couple of good **Hmmms!** This is a time for implementation; this is a time for action. Your leadership is needed right now, and if not you . . . who? This is your time, so don't wait in line. STEP TO THE FRONT AND LEAD!

Hmmm #10

Excuses are Just Reasons in Disguise

Many times in order to overcome a problem or hurdle, you must first thoroughly understand what it is. So let's define an excuse. The *Merriam-Webster Dictionary* defines *excuse* (as a verb) in several ways:

1. to make apology;
2. to pardon;
3. to release from an obligation; and
4. to justify.

Do any of these ring a bell? I think it's safe to say at some point in our lives we've all done some—if not all—of these things. Now, for the Gregg Amerman definition, which is a little more substantial: I believe excuses are self-imposed stop signs that keep us from completing our journeys to financial freedom and personal fulfillment. In other words, they negate responsibility and allow us to feel okay with where we are instead of where we should be.

Of course, excuses play a huge part in our daily lives. They've been around since the beginning of mankind. In fact, let's go back, I mean waaaaaaaaaaay back, to the Garden of Eden. That's pretty far back. In Genesis, after Adam took a bite of the forbidden fruit and then was asked by God if he'd eaten off the tree he was commanded not to eat from, Adam unleashed the world's first excuse: "The woman who thou gavest to be with me, she gave me of the tree, and I did eat." Eve quickly chimed in with her own excuse when God asked what she'd done: "The serpent beguiled me, and I did eat" (King James Version). Right there, excuses were born. While they both had the chance to take responsibility for their own actions, Adam and Eve simply justified them. Well, here we are eons later and excuses still remain as our primary mechanism against lack of action, follow through, production, and results.

Every single person on the face of this planet has been guilty of making excuses in some form of another. Me. You. Your boss. Your spouse. Your friends. Your parents. Your coworkers. Your children. Your students. Your peers. Your vendors. Your teammates. Your clients. For years, I've said I need to get in better shape, yet have I made an honest commitment to doing so? Not until just recently.

But just how big of an impact do excuses play in our lives? Well, for those who are successful at reaching their goals, those excuses are converted into motivation by the obstacles that caused the excuses in the first place. But those who struggle to reach their goals do so because these obstacles and the excuses that follow stop them.

So let's find out more about who you are and which excuses are your favorites. See the following list of common excuses and check off the ones you've used to keep yourself, and possibly others, from achieving goals. Or from fulfilling your potential. Or led to you missing the chance to change your life.

Go ahead—what are you waiting for? Check the boxes of the excuses you've used before—or maybe just yesterday or today. Notice that the check boxes are in the shape of stop signs as a reminder of all the many instances we have literally stopped our progress and got caught up in life's proverbial traffic jam. Successful people don't sit in traffic very often; they know the right roads to take and stop signs to them are just yield signs to make sure they are going the right way.

○ I have no money.
○ I have no time.
○ I don't know the right people.
○ Nobody's hiring.
○ The economy is bad.
○ Nobody likes me.
○ I can't catch a break.
○ I was given bad advice.
○ I'm not healthy enough.

○ I can't do it.
○ I have difficult relationships.
○ Trouble just seems to find me.
○ I had a hard childhood.
○ It's impossible.
○ I have children.
○ I'm not popular enough.
○ I live in a bad neighborhood.

○ It's too big of a risk.
○ I'm too old.
○ I'm too young.
○ I can't afford to do it.
○ It's always something.
○ People always tell me no.
○ I'm not talented enough.
○ I don't know how.
○ I don't have enough education.
○ I don't have enough support.
○ My job is too stressful.
○ It never works out for me.
○ I was lied to and misled.
○ I have no confidence.
○ I'm not outgoing enough.
○ This is different than I'm used to.
○ My spouse won't let me.
○ I have a mortgage payment.
○ I have too many family obligations.
○ I don't have a family.
○ I have too much housework.
○ I'm still working towards retirement.
○ My boss doesn't like me.
○ My business isn't successful enough.
○ It's too much work.
○ They're prejudiced against me.
○ I'm not that kind of person.
○ Other _____
○ Other _____

So, do you have a few stop signs in your life? Now, before you start thinking I'm some kind of cold-hearted person with no feelings, understanding, or compassion for the realities in life, you're missing the point. I make excuses too; however, I ultimately turn those excuses into reasons. Believe me—I realize that the excuses listed in these two columns might very well be true for you, and it's obvious that if these are your circumstances and challenges, it's not easy. But whoever said life was easy? No matter who you are, at some point you're going to face obstacles and difficult conditions. One thing holds true for all of them: you still have a choice in how you approach them.

Your choice is this: you can decide to make your excuses legitimate and valid so that you believe they're not excuses but instead facts for why you are where you are. Your legitimate excuses are the barriers that hold you back from achieving true success. Your legitimate excuses will keep you limited financially, unhappy, and unfulfilled. But by choosing to seize the moment and realize that excuses are just reasons in disguise, you can produce financial freedom, success, and fulfillment.

So, what's it going to be—an excuse or a reason? I know if you're reading this book, the answer is obvious. Let's give you some strategies to accomplish this.

1. *It's either reasons or regrets.*

    Have you ever had regrets before? How did that make you feel? Regrets are the worst. You find yourself playing the same scenario over and over again in your head with all the things you could have done, should have done, and would have done, but one thing hasn't changed: the result. Realize that excuses lead to regrets and reasons lead to effort, and with effort comes the satisfaction that you gave it everything you got. Even if you don't succeed at the level you hoped, you still feel good about who you are, with no regrets about what could have been. Like many great athletes say, "Leave it all out on the field."

2. *Accept the fact that there will always be something.*

Sure, some of your excuses are indeed legitimate—your roof needs to be fixed and your car needs to be serviced and your mortgage needs to be paid and your boss might be hard to deal with and you have to pay off your debt. But that doesn't mean these obstacles can't be overcome. Yes, it often seems like there's "always something." But if you let yourself get bogged down by the "always somethings," you'll find your goals and dreams will be "forever nothings."

3. *Find the value and make them things you need to do.*

What's most important to you right now? Improving your finances? Having better relationships? Securing a promotion? Building a business? Spending more time with your family? Excuse making is often the result of not having enough value combined with only things you want to do. When this is the case, it tends to be all too easy to justify and make excuses, like when your friends invite you to go out when you know you should be preparing for a big presentation or closing out a sales month that could earn you a high-paying promotion. When there is serious value at stake, deadlines in place, and a need to accomplish the task, it's much harder to succumb to an excuse. And in most cases, you will use your excuses as the reasons to forge ahead.

4. *Focus on can, not can't.*

In my household the word *can't* doesn't come up very often. *Can't* is the easiest excuse in the book and simply means you don't even need to give it a shot. Therefore, we always focus on what we can do, not what we can't do. Imagine driving home one evening and coming upon some unexpected construction, closing off the road you usually take home. Do you say, "Well, now I can't get home, so I guess I'll just pull into a parking lot and sleep in my car tonight"? Of course not. You would just find another way to your house. Why? Because your immediate expectation is that you can get home, just not the same way you usually go. And this is how you need to approach everything in your life, personally and professionally. No matter what happens, you must display and believe in an "I can" attitude. Believing you can is the predominant part of turning your excuses into reasons.

5. *Accept the ultimate responsibility—you write the story of your life.*

Throughout your life, there will be many instances, circumstances, and situations beyond your control. But the majority of them *will* be directly in your control and directly related to the choices and decisions *you* make. So when you make a mistake or drop the ball or just flat-out screw up, don't assign blame or start rattling off all the excuses for why. Just hold yourself accountable, admit to your mistake, and take responsibility. Then, when the initial sting wears off, ask yourself what you learned from your mistake. And most importantly, don't do it again! Always spend your time figuring out solutions, making adjustments, and seeking alternatives, instead of concocting excuses. Over the long haul, your life story will be written by you. While you may not be able to erase anything you've written, you always have a chance and can find a reason to turn to a fresh page and begin writing a new chapter.

6. *Use your excuses as reasons and action motivators.*

Below you will see the same list of excuses we examined earlier to identify some of our most commonly used excuses. The difference is that each one has been converted into a reason and a motivation to take action. So the big **hmmm** here is every time you come up with an excuse, spend a few minutes converting it to your reason, which is how you will overcome, conquer, and continue to move forward toward your goals.

EXCUSE: I have no money.

REASON: How many times by this point in your life have you said, "I have no money"? Isn't it obvious that anyone who believes they have no money will never take the course of action to have money? Why is it that the people who have the least are afraid to lose the most, and the people who have the most are afraid to lose the least? Who knows how many opportunities you've missed because you're afraid to lose something you don't even have. Always remember, most people are so afraid to lose what they have they'll never get what they want. If you want more money, don't chase it! If you chase it, it will elude you. Focus instead on personal growth and developing the right mindset and skill-set of someone who makes money. (As a side note: isn't it amazing how we always find money for things we need? Make success something you need!) And, finally, ask yourself, do you like having no money? How long have you had no money, and how long do you want to have no money? I think you have a good reason to make some money!

EXCUSE: I have no time.

REASON: We all have time. What you don't have is value for that time. Once you place value on whatever it is you want to accomplish, you'll make the time to get it done. Then the only thing left to do is effectively manage your time.

EXCUSE: I don't know the right people.

REASON: It doesn't matter how many of the right people you know. The key is how many of the right people know you. Work on becoming a professional communicator and building relationships with influential people. Realize that your network equals your net worth.

EXCUSE: Nobody's hiring.

REASON: Great! What an excellent time to start your own business career. Now you have no excuses—it couldn't be a better time. In addition, you can use this time to sharpen some of your existing skills or to learn some new skills for a career change.

EXCUSE: I can't catch a break.

REASON: Remember thoughts are things, so the more you say you can't catch a break, the more it *appears* you can't catch a break. Why don't you rephrase it and say, "There is zero doubt in my mind that I'm going to catch a break!" Oh, by the way, the key to catching a break is consistency, loving what you do, having a strong work ethic, and great time management skills. These ingredients are a perfect recipe for the break you're looking for.

EXCUSE: I'm not healthy enough.

REASON: Well, it's good that you realize it because, regardless of the success you have in your life, if you're not healthy to enjoy it, what's the point of having it in the first place? It's seems pretty simple to me: Focus on your health. Seek the proper health recommendations and make the necessary changes and adjustments to your lifestyle to become healthier than you've ever been. Then, not only will you have the vitality, energy, and desire to pursue your goals, you will feel great. Wow! What a great opportunity—the chance to get healthy!

EXCUSE: I can't do it.

REASON: Think about all the times you approached a task saying "I can't do it," only to ultimately complete the task and feel great about your accomplishment. As long as it's been done by one other person, if not many more, it's possible and can be done. But you also have to realize that there have been many men and woman throughout the course of history who were the first in their particular endeavor. The easiest thing to say when that "I can't do it" pops into your head is to say, "I'll give it my best effort." That's all you can do anyway, and what you'll find by taking this approach is that you *can* accomplish much more than you think!

EXCUSE: I have difficult relationships.

REASON: Remember, you are half of all those relationships. So either you need to accept responsibility for making those relationships difficult and make the changes necessary to improve them, or you need to confront the issues with others. At the end of the day, you can only control you. So if you come to the conclusion through your best effort that you can't change the people around you, then change the people around you. In other words, either become a better friend or find better friends to have relationships with.

EXCUSE: Trouble just seems to find me.

REASON: I assure you, if you're always in trouble, it's because you associate with the wrong people. You are whom you hang out with. So start hanging out with people who don't get into trouble, and miraculously trouble will stop finding you.

EXCUSE: I had a hard childhood.

REASON: Remember what I said earlier: Don't focus on what you can't do, only on what you can do. None of us can change the past. I wish there was a way I could erase all of the challenging times you had as a child, but the reality is I can't. Neither can you. But what you can do is focus on allowing those past moments to define your strength and character, enabling you to overcome current challenges and achieve greatness in spite of your hard childhood.

One of my mentors and great friends, Dr. Ramie Tritt, had a verbally and physically abusive father. Dr. Tritt could have easily allowed that to be his excuse for never living up to his full potential. But he chose to rise above his past and found a reason to become a highly successful surgeon and entrepreneur, and more importantly, a wonderful spouse and parent. Dr. Tritt is among countless people who had challenging childhoods and one of the many success stories who turned a difficult past into a great present.

Finally, you've got a chance to do something special. Not only can you be a shining example of what can be, regardless of your past circumstances, but you can also be an inspiration to others.

EXCUSE: It's impossible.

REASON: It really depends on what we're talking about. If you're saying it's impossible to live without air, I'd agree with you. If you said the NY Jets were going to be the 2005 Super Bowl champions, I would have said, "That is impossible." If you said I was going to be twenty years old again, although I would love it, I would have said, again, "Impossible."

Beyond ridiculous notions like these, most things are not impossible. They may not be probable, but as long as there is any degree of possibility, big or small, it's certainly possible. Can you imagine if Thomas Edison, the Wright brothers, Henry Ford, Martin Luther King Jr., and many other great inventors and leaders thought it were impossible to have light, fly, drive, and enjoy newfound personal freedoms? Think about what the world would be missing out on today. I don't know what you're working on that would make you feel it's impossible, but I'm pretty confident that if we can send a person to the moon, it's possible you can achieve your goals. As I stated earlier in referencing Napoleon Hill, "What the mind of man can conceive and believe, the mind can achieve." If you thought it, it's no longer impossible!

EXCUSE: I have children.

REASON: This is an easy one. How could you possibly look your kids in the face one day and blame them for all the things you didn't accomplish that would have dramatically impacted your life, their life, and their future? This is your chance to lead by example by passionately pursuing your dreams. Living a fulfilling, successful, satisfying life, and, ultimately, achieving your goals will make you a much better and more respected parent. You owe it to yourself and your children, so never view your kids as an excuse. Always view them as a reason!

EXCUSE: I'm not popular enough.

REASON: There is a huge difference between being popular and being loved. Popularity is way overrated because it is not real. In other words, most of the time when you are popular it's not because of genuine and sincere feelings. Popularity causes people to know you for what you've done, not who you are, and those are not the type of relationships that will bring value to your life. Popularity oftentimes goes as fast as it comes. Love, however, can last a lifetime. So, instead of focusing on popularity, focus on love. Take a great lesson out of the movie classic *The Wizard of Oz*, when the Wizard said to the Tin Man, "A heart is not judged by how much you love but by how much you are loved by others." And by the way, when you focus on being loved first, popularity usually comes along with it.

EXCUSE: It's too big of a risk.

REASON: Risk is a matter of interpretation. Pretend for a minute that you're sixty-five years old and you've worked hard for forty years. As you retire, you are now dependent on your pension, investments, and/or social security. You may be forced to downsize and reduce your current lifestyle that you worked so hard to create, or you may just have to keep working to stay afloat.

Now, wouldn't you consider that the ultimate risk? Of course, you want to be smart about the risks you take, but at the end of the day, risk is exciting, risk is challenging, risk brings the passion and desire out of any individual. Risk is what creates great opportunities. But doing nothing to increase your wealth, health, and happiness for later in life—now that's the biggest risk you'll ever take.

EXCUSE: I'm too old.

REASON: If your goal is to play professional basketball in the NBA, then I'd have to agree with you. But it wouldn't be because of your age—it would be because of your lack of reality.

Obviously there are certain things that your age limits; however, there are far more things that your age has no bearing on. You're never too old to become who or what you want to be. You're never too old to achieve wealth, to have success or fulfillment. It's never too late to redefine yourself.

Take Colonel Sanders, founder of world-famous Kentucky Fried Chicken. When the Colonel was six, his father died, leaving him to care for his baby brother and sister. As he got older, he held a series of jobs. He was a farmer, streetcar conductor, soldier, railroad fireman, studied law, sold insurance, operated an Ohio River steamboat ferry, sold tires, and operated service stations. And after all of these jobs, he arrived at age sixty-five, reduced to living on his $105 Social Security checks.

But this was his starting point. With nothing to his name, the Colonel devoted himself to the chicken franchising business. He drove across the country from restaurant to restaurant, cooking batches of chicken for restaurant owners and their employees until his recipe finally caught on. Now the Kentucky Fried Chicken business he started has grown to be one of the largest retail food service systems in the world. More than two billion KFC dinners are served annually in more than eighty-two countries around the world. Colonel Sanders not only became a quick service restaurant pioneer but an actual symbol of entrepreneurial spirit. Could you imagine if Colonels Sanders thought he was too old? None of us would have ever experienced his "finger-licking good" chicken.

Too old? The only thing too old is your stinking thinking! Regardless of where you are, as soon as you're ready, you can change where you're going.

EXCUSE: I'm too young.

REASON: Be thankful for this moment in time: I'm sure Colonel Sanders would have loved to trade places with you. The only downside to the Colonel's age was that he didn't have more time to enjoy what he built. You, on the other hand, have infinite possibilities. Have you been cut off from world news? Have you not seen teenagers becoming entrepreneurs, millionaires, and even billionaires? This is the most extraordinary time—entrepreneurship and the accumulation of wealth have no age limitations!

But let's get beyond just money. As we discussed in an earlier **hmmm**, your time, and therefore your youth, is the most limited resource you have. Please don't squander this very valuable time as an excuse. You of all people should have the greatest reason of all—being young won't last long. The tremendous value of youth versus wealth would best be described by the late Joan B. Kroc, wife of McDonald's CEO Ray Kroc. When a young person wished they could trade places with the billionaire, Mrs. Kroc stated that she wished she could too and that she would be getting the better of the deal. She would have taken youth over money in a heartbeat. Take advantage of your youth. It's the number one thing everyone who's older wished they had. Take immediate action now because youth is not only a reason— it's an advantage!

EXCUSE: I can't afford to do it.

REASON: Can you afford to stay in the circumstances you're in now? I tend to doubt it, because if you could, this wouldn't even be on your excuse list. The funniest part about this excuse is that the people who say they can't afford it are the ones who can't afford *not* to do it. I can really relate to this one because I thought the same thing at one point. But let me share how I went from living in a room in someone else's house, being three months behind on my car payment, and having a minus sign in front of the numbers in my checking account. It's three sets of three words: "Want it bad, find a way, make it happen." Believe me, I couldn't afford anything, but I couldn't afford to stay where I was any longer either. So, want it bad, find a way, and make it happen, and ultimately you'll have afforded yourself an opportunity of a lifetime.

EXCUSE: It's always something.

REASON: It will always be something, and it will almost never be the right time. While planning is an important ingredient for success, many times things just happen beyond your control, altering your game plan. So the question becomes, do you wait to do all the things you've always wanted to do, waiting to get "all your ducks in a row" or for the stars, moon, and sun to align? If so, you could be waiting a long time and therefore could miss out on countless opportunities, experiences, and dreams. Don't wait too long to forge a special relationship, to have children, and most importantly, to pursue your dreams. Remember the hourglass from an earlier **hmmm**? Well, the sands of time are slipping away. Don't let your goals and dreams do the same.

EXCUSE: People always tell me no.

REASON: That's good, because you'll get to the yeses that much sooner. The only reason there is gratification in accomplishing something is that there are challenges, obstacles, and rejections to overcome, get around, or get through. What would baseball be like if they just lobbed the ball directly over the plate to the batters? Or in football if the quarterback handed the ball off to the running back and the defense just moved out of the way to let him run by, or in hockey the goalies just decided to vacate the net? What if each hole on a golf course was five hundred feet in diameter? None of this would hold the interest of the players or the fans very long.

Of course, it would be great if everyone wanted to buy what we were selling, do what we were doing, or said yes to everything we were asking. But if that were the case, there would be no reason to work hard, improve, or strive to be the best. Realize that you'll never get more yeses than nos, but you need far less yeses than nos to be immensely successful.

EXCUSE: I'm not talented enough.

REASON: "Talented" is what other people say you are, not how you should define your success. You don't get anything for being talented; you achieve because you produce results. In addition, talent is less about something you have and more about something you obtain. If you're willing to spend the time, energy, and resources to learn and perfect a skill, people will say you're talented. Instead of looking at what you're not talented at, surround yourself with people who are more talented than you in the areas that are not your strengths. From the lips of billionaire J. Paul Getty, "I would rather have 1 percent of 100 people's effort than 100 percent of my own." So the question is would you rather be talented or successful? Don't worry about talent, focus on results!

EXCUSE: I don't know how.

REASON: You didn't know how to read, you didn't know how to tie your shoes, you didn't know how to get dressed, you didn't know how to drive—couldn't we go on for days with all the things we didn't know how to do? Yet today you can do all those things you once said you didn't know how to do. And the way you learned all of these things you do on a daily basis will work for anything you want to know. Here is the four-step process we used to learn countless things throughout our lives, a process that will work for you again right now.

1. Start with someone telling you. People who have successfully already done what you're attempting to do can tell you exactly what they did.

2. Once they tell you, they then simultaneously show you. This is even more powerful, because just being told leaves a lot for interpretation. Being shown how to do something makes less room for error and gives the person being shown more confidence in the next step.

3. Try to do what you were told and shown. As you begin putting this info to use, you'll make mistakes because it's new and uncomfortable. But over time with more telling, showing, adjustments, and practice, you eventually can do it.

4. Do it. Once you've practiced it enough times, you now have the confidence to do it and, not only are you doing it, but you're now in a position to take other people through the four-step process.

Well, that excuse is gone, now you only have a reason because now you know how to know how.

Okay. I've done enough of the work here. It's time for you to take over. I've done my job, steps one and two from above. I've told you how, and I've shown you how. Now you have to attempt doing what you were told and shown. Below are the remaining excuses from the original checklist. Turn these excuses into reasons and motivations and write down the benefits you can gain from these excuses you turned into reasons.

EXCUSE: I don't have enough education.

REASON:

EXCUSE: I don't have enough support.

REASON:

EXCUSE: My job is too stressful.

REASON:

EXCUSE: It never works out for me.

REASON:

EXCUSE: I was lied to and misled.

REASON:

EXCUSE: I have no confidence.

REASON:

EXCUSE: I'm not outgoing enough.

REASON:

EXCUSE: This is different than I'm used to.

REASON:

EXCUSE: I'm not that kind of person.

REASON:

EXCUSE: My spouse won't let me.

REASON:

EXCUSE: I have a mortgage payment.

REASON:

EXCUSE: I have too many family obligations.

REASON:

EXCUSE: I don't have a family.

REASON:

EXCUSE: I have too much housework.

REASON:

EXCUSE: I'm still working towards retirement.

REASON:

EXCUSE: My boss doesn't like me.

REASON:

EXCUSE: My business isn't successful enough.

REASON:

EXCUSE: It's too much work.

REASON:

EXCUSE: They're prejudiced against me.

REASON:

So, how did you do? Was it difficult or uncomfortable to convert these excuses into reasons? Remember, your success starts in your head, with your thoughts and attitudes. Doing this exercise will train your mind to find reasons instead of excuses, which will help you achieve the success you desire.

At the end of the day, we can all find an excuse for why we're not doing more, achieving more, changing more, and earning more. But I'm sure you can recall a time in your life when you went above and beyond, pushed the limits, did whatever it took, even though it was difficult, unpleasant, grueling, or painful—all because you needed something *that bad*, or in some cases, because your life depended on it. And those specific instances simply revolve around things in our lives that have tremendous value.

So, recognize excuses for what they are—stop signs on your road to success—and start converting them into valuable reasons today. Once you do that, you'll start realizing you're living your life the best way possible: on your terms, with no excuses and no regrets.

"SUCCESS: When a want becomes a need...that's when you'll succeed!**"**

Hmmm #11

We'll See Philosophy

In a classic confrontation from the movie *A Few Good Men*, Lt. Daniel Kaffee (Tom Cruise) and Col. Nathan Jessup (Jack Nicholson) square off against each other in the courtroom. Kaffee shouts, "I want the truth!" and Jessup yells back, "You can't handle the truth!" Well, while it may be true that, like Kaffee, we all want the truth and that Jessup was right—that many people can't handle the truth—one other truth holds true: most people don't tell the truth! (Try saying that five times fast.) So, with that in mind, consider two words I use often: *We'll see!*

Now, I don't want to come across as a cynic or a pessimist—because, believe me, I'm the biggest of dreamers and most people probably consider me an eternal optimist—but through my experiences in life and business, I've learned to become a realist in my expectations of others.

Since we're talking about truth, which is synonymous with honesty, the first thing we have to be is honest with ourselves. In many of the seminars I've conducted over the years, I've asked the audience if they've ever lied. Of course, many hands go up but numerous hands don't get raised, which then prompts me to say, "You're a liar." It's always good for a laugh, let's be honest—this is a book about a true awakening and if now is not the time to awaken to the fact that we lie to others, and worse—we lie to ourselves—when will be a good time? You see, the problem for many of us is we only consider a lie to be something with bad intent or was premeditated. We don't consider it a lie to tell someone you'll call them right back and then don't call them at all, to make an appointment with someone and then not show up or even call them, or to promise something and then not deliver on that promise. Whether you want to believe it or not, these are all lies. They may not have malicious intent or ill will but they are still impacting the decisions, perceptions, and lives of others.

Now, the lesson here is not to become a raging pessimist who looks for the worst in everyone. That's not the case at all. Instead, be a realist. After spending nearly two decades in the business world, I've come to the conclusion that the vast majority of people do not do what they say they're going to do. They don't follow through. They talk but they don't act. Mark Twain had it dead right when he said, "Actions speak louder than words, but not nearly as often."

No matter who you are, no matter what you do, I'm sure you can relate to this phenomenon. I'm sure you've been disappointed more than once—probably lots of times—by someone not coming through with something they've said they were going to do. People will say things for a number of reasons:

to impress you, to get you off their back, to make themselves look good, to sell you something, to try to make a deal with you. People just spout things off, and they really don't have an appreciation for how important it is to follow through instead of just talking. And this can lead to a range of unpleasant situations for you, from basic, day-to-day frustrations to major, big-time disappointments that can affect your life.

Of course, I didn't always have this philosophical view on things. I used to be idealistic and probably to some degree just naïve, but I believed that what came out of people's mouths was as good as gold. Ha! Was I ever wrong! I can recall countless times, especially early in my career, when someone made some kind of statement, promise, or commitment. Gregg, just come to my city, I'll have hundreds of people for you to talk to! Gregg, I'm going to be the best producer you've ever seen. Gregg, I'm going to introduce you to the best person you've ever met. Gregg, I've got an *incredible* deal for you! Gregg, I know a way you can make millions! Gregg, you better clear your calendar because you're going to be so busy. Gregg, I'm going to have that money back to you on this exact date. Gregg, I'm going to give you a percentage of the company. Gregg, I want you to make a lot of money.

At first, all of these things were exciting to hear. I mean, who wouldn't want all of these things, right? I would get so motivated and be so enthusiastic, because in my mind these things were happening; that's what these people told me, right? So for days, weeks, or even months, I would be counting on these things to come to fruition and often making decisions and taking actions that overextended myself, both financially and personally, and even jeopardizing my own good word. But, eventually, the disappointments started stacking up. Over and over, I'd get all fired up about one of these so-called opportunities. And over and over, I wasted my time, my eagerness, my money, and my efforts on deals that fell through, plans that never came to completion and words that never became reality. I can't tell you how many times I heard, "You have my word," only to have that word mean nothing. Eventually, I got tired of getting my hopes up, only to watch them crash time and time again. So ultimately, when people started coming to me with their big ideas, their grand plans, and all the things they said they were going to do, I started saying those two little magic words: *We'll see.*

Wouldn't it be great if people were like Pinocchio, and every time they lied, their noses grew? It would be a lot easier to identify whom to trust, whom to do business with, and whom to count on. But unfortunately, if this were the reality, you probably couldn't stand squarely in front of most people because you would be speared every time they opened their mouth. So, since a rapidly growing nose isn't an option, how else can we tell if people are lying? It's simple: If their lips move. In other words, *you can't listen to what people say, you have to watch what they do.* Now, there are always exceptions to the rule, and in this case, the exception is the relationship, history, and track record of the individual making the claim. If you have positive experiences with this person—they follow through and their record is sparkling—then you are less likely to be disappointed by their outcome. However, I still believe in the notion that it's better to err on the side of *we'll see* than to count your chickens before they hatch. It's okay to be optimistic, encouraged, and to have a good feeling about things, but don't celebrate until it's official. You'll save yourself a tremendous amount of aggravation, disappointment, and frustration if you just respond to the outcome instead of the talk.

In utilizing the *we'll see* philosophy, it's really important to keep several things in mind. My points here are not to discourage you from trusting people and/or opportunities or to make you bitter based upon past disappointments but merely to do three things: Evaluate the intent, good or bad; keep things in the proper perspective; and keep your good word and reputation stellar.

1. *Evaluate the intent: Is it good or bad?*

For example: You call the customer service department of your cell phone company about a charge on your bill you didn't rack up, and the service agent assures you it will be taken care of on your next bill. And guess what? That bill comes around again next month, and that charge is still there. Here's an instance where you could have said *we'll see* because you wouldn't really know if the agent handled your situation properly until you received the next bill. But it's highly unlikely that the customer service agent had bad intent, more likely just incompetence. So, it would really be no big deal, because by saying *we'll see*, you were doing just that, waiting to see. All you would be doing here is calling them back to get it handled.

On the other hand, let's say you accepted a job with a new company, and the factor that seals you taking it is that they promise you you'll be running the department in no time. But five years later, you're still in the exact same position. There is certainly the possibility of bad intent, especially if they told you that just so they could land you for the job. But if you had had a *we'll see* philosophy, you wouldn't have been surprised after a shorter period of time, and you would be certain to inquire about their failure to deliver on their promise. Or you would have had them put it in writing prior to accepting the job. In most cases, people would have been so excited about their promising future that they might have prematurely told other people about their upcoming promotion and even done things prematurely and in the end left the job because of the false promises and unfulfilled expectations. The great part about the *we'll see* philosophy is it makes you think more about covering all of your bases in advance because you know people don't always do what they say.

2.   *Keep things in proper perspective.*

My example here is a personal experience. In the past twenty years, I have had numerous dealings with various builders and contractors for residential and commercial properties. While some did better work and were easier to work with than others, one characteristic was the same: not one of them ever delivered in the time frame they promised. The worst experience I had was getting my mom's house built. From top to bottom, this company was the absolute worst. Everything they could do wrong, they did; everything they promised to do, they failed to deliver. It took them four times just to deliver the right bricks. Pathetic! But the *we'll see* philosophy saved us because we didn't just accept their word or promises—we had it all documented and in writing. In addition, because we said *we'll see*, we waited until the house was completely finished before we made arrangements for my mom to move in, which meant she wasn't terribly inconvenienced by their poor time projections. In the end, it took six months longer than what was originally discussed and yet it didn't affect us at all. But boy, we celebrated when that house was finally finished!

Another great example of keeping things in the proper perspective is the world of sports. There are so many highs and lows in one single game. I remember going to an Atlanta Falcons football game with my good friend and attorney Earle Burke, and to say he is a loyal, diehard fan is an understatement. So here I am sitting at the game, and there must have been at least seventy thousand frenzied fans in the stands. As the visiting team kicked off, the Falcons fans were standing in anticipation of a big return, but as the return man caught the ball and started running, he was immediately hit, fumbling the football. After a scramble, the visiting team grabbed it up and ran it in for a touchdown.

You should have seen and heard how quickly the wind came out of the fans' sails. It was silent, like everyone had just lost a loved one. I remember saying to Earle, "It's no big deal, *we'll see* what happens." Only a minute had gone off the clock so there was plenty of time left to win the game.

Anyway, the teams set up for another kickoff, and the fans began to come back to life. This time the kick returner fielded the ball, no problem, and the offense came out. The crowd was roaring again, and on the first play, the quarterback threw an interception that was returned for a touchdown. Talk about déjà-vu. It was like the crowd went into a simultaneous state of depression. Again, I thought, *we'll see* what happens. Well, ultimately the Falcons came back and won the game, and all I kept thinking about were those huge swings of unnecessary emotions. If they just would have waited to see the outcome, they never would have had all that stress and worry about what was happening at those few early mishaps with the rest of the game remaining to be played.

Think about how many times you've witnessed or actually felt it yourself. Think about a big football game, one with playoff implications. One team is trailing by a few points, and with the clock winding down, they drive down the field and score a touchdown to pull ahead. And of course, the fans, and most times even the players, are celebrating like crazy, like they've already won the game—even though there's plenty of time left for the other team to score! And oftentimes we see just that happen—that's the name of the game in sports. And then the fans who were going nuts a few minutes ago are ten times more disappointed than they would have been had they not gotten their hopes up in the first place. It's almost as entertaining as the game itself!

But the key is to watch the coach. They're not showing much emotion because they know all about *we'll see.* Just remember, *we'll see* allows you to wait for the finish.

3.   *Keep your good word and reputation stellar.*

The notion of *we'll see* goes beyond just how we view others in relation to their follow through. Consider the domino effect of putting too much stock in what others say instead of what they do. Let's say you're a sales rep and you meet a new customer who says he's going to buy ten thousand of your new widgets. Now, there's nothing official yet, but you shake on the deal after your lunch meeting, and you practically float back to your office thinking about that fat commission check heading your way. You dash into your supervisor's office and tell him, "I just sold ten thousand widgets!" He congratulates you and slaps you on the back. Soon, word gets around the office about your amazing deal, and for the rest of the day, you're the star of the office. A week later, you're still flying high. That is, until you get a phone call from your customer who tells you, because of some cutbacks to his budget, he won't be able to buy those ten thousand widgets after all, so sorry, but he'll keep you in mind for next time. Now, you have to go back to the powers that be and explain the situation. And then hope that you won't lose your job or die of embarrassment once the rest of the office finds out, or worse, won't have cost your company money and resources because they geared up for this big order and counted on that revenue to meet their budget.

And to think, all of this angst could have been prevented—or, at the very least, lessened—with the *we'll see* philosophy. If you'd waited to get a signed contract before telling anyone about the sale. If you'd held off on imagining the vacation you'd take with the commission. If you'd not planned anything before you knew it was a done deal, instead of one that sounded good and had potential. Everything has potential, but we're not looking for potential—we're looking for results. So *we'll see!*

All of this is not to say you shouldn't celebrate over small victories. My point is that you shouldn't count on something as final until it's official, because time and time again, people will let you down with what they say. So don't announce victory until the bill has been corrected. Until the deal has been signed. Until the order has been placed. Until the sale has been made. Until the promotion has been achieved. Until the raise kicks in. Until the house has been built. Until someone establishes a track record of delivering on their promises to you. Until that happens, here's the attitude that should prevail: *We'll see.*

And here's why I feel so strongly about this: I think if *we'll see* was an integral part of everyone's vocabularies, we'd have a lot less disappointment, discouragement, frustration, lost time, and wasted energy in our lives. And I don't just mean from how we would personally feel but also by us not making other people feel this way. You see, there's a bigger picture here. *We'll see* is a phrase that can prevent you from committing too soon, making a false promise, over promising and under delivering, or providing premature information.

When you think about it, parents are masters of saying *we'll see* to their children. Can we go to Disney World soon? *We'll see.* Can I have a bike for my birthday? *We'll see.* Can we visit the zoo this weekend? *We'll see.* Parents know better than to promise what they can't deliver to their children, so instead of saying *yes* to those wishes they may not be able to deliver on just yet, they say *we'll see.* That way, there are no dashed hopes, no unfulfilled expectations, no disappointments. After all, kids never forget, and good parents never want to be the reason for their kids' unhappiness.

I remember hearing *we'll see* often enough as a child. And as I've grown to be a successful adult in the business world, as well as having my own family, I realized those two words could also serve me well, just as they'd served my parents when my brothers and I were kids. So the essential **hmmm** here is in knowing you do not want to be disappointed, let down, or worse—lied to—so make sure you don't do it to others. The best plan is to be brutally honest. In today's world, it is very difficult to know who or what to trust, and the days of having multiple chances to prove yourself are over. You have very little room for error. Don't take the risk by embellishing and stretching the truth just to close a deal, make a sale, or get someone to do something. Remember, that person is counting on your honesty and your truths to make a decision. And whether it's a small or a big one, they deserve the truth. That's why I love *we'll see*, because it's the truth!

Of course, I'm not suggesting that you say *we'll see* every time every single person in your life tells you something. That would not be a very conducive way to establishing or maintaining strong relationships with people. You'll find people out there who will do what they say, time and time again. I can think of numerous people in my life, especially within my inner circle, to whom I very rarely have to say *we'll see* because they've all proven themselves to follow up on what they say they'll do. Some people might refer to this as having a strong character; others might say it's integrity or dependability. Whatever the case, these are the kind of people you should surround yourself with in life: those to whom you don't need to say *we'll see*.

But how will you know right off the bat whether people will follow through with what they say they will? You don't. It takes time for people to prove themselves. Until then, all you should do is say *we'll see*. *We'll see* applies most when you're getting to know someone, when you're just beginning a relationship, and when you're witnessing for the first time what they can and will do.

Furthermore, when expectations are even higher for someone to perform well, you need to incorporate *we'll see* even more. Think about a job interview, for example. Most people don't show up to a job interview and act like a complete imbecile, do they? No. Most of the time they dress for success, put their best foot forward, talk about their strengths, and sell themselves as best they can to get the job. But it's impossible to tell how they'll really do in their new position until they're actually in their new position. Until then? *We'll see.*

The bottom line: that phrase "My word is my bond" needs to be changed to "My action is my bond." And until you see the results, you should be using *we'll see* a lot more often. Again, think of the frustration, discouragement, wasted time and efforts, and disappointment you'll save for yourself.

The *we'll see* philosophy is also applicable with respect to commitments (or lack thereof) to yourself. How? Well, consider how many times you've made a personal vow to yourself. That you'll join a gym. Or quit smoking. Or get out of debt. Or lose weight. Or travel to new places. Or find a new job. Or start a new business. Or any number of other personal goals you may have set for yourself. But, when those statements and commitments are constantly unfulfilled, what happens more often than not? Without realizing it, we've got people in our lives saying *we'll see* to us and, even worse, we're saying *we'll see* to ourselves.

I probably don't have to tell you at this point that *we'll see* is not a good thing to be hearing from yourself or from people around you. Maybe they don't even exactly say the words *we'll see*, but they communicate it regardless. Maybe by grunting. Or saying *umm hmmm*. Or just nodding absent-mindedly. Whatever the case, this isn't a reaction you're looking for in your relationships with other people. It means you've become a fixture of unreliability, whether that's in respect to what you're saying you'll do for yourself or for someone else.

It all goes back to a lack of follow through, which is another critical aspect to the *we'll see* philosophy. If people would just *do* what they *say* they're going to do, there would be no need to say *we'll see*! But that's not the case. You can have the best intentions in the world, with all your dreams, desires, and goals all laid out for yourself and your life. But if you don't follow through with them, none of that matters. Life doesn't change because you have a dream or a goal. Life changes with the follow through. With the doing. With matching the walk with the talk. Action, after all, is vastly different from intention. On the flip side, not having people or yourself thinking or saying *we'll see* in relation to your statements, promises, and commitments is one of the greatest compliments of all. It's saying you can be believed in, that you can be counted on, and that you're going to make it happen. That's certainly something to strive for.

So, let me ask you this: Are the things you're reading in this book making you go **hmmm**? Is there an awakening taking place? I mean, do you really want to change your life? Do you really want to discover financial freedom? Maybe start a new career or business for yourself? Achieve personal and professional growth? Build stronger relationships? Lead a happier, more successful life? Do you have your goals set, and now you're ready to actually take action to get there? Is that a yes? I believe I can almost hear you saying, Yes, *I'm shooting for my goals in life, Gregg! And I'm really going to do it this time!*

And you probably already know what I'm saying back to you: That's great, but you know my favorite two words . . . we'll see!

"POTENTIAL: People love to throw around the word 'potential,' like it gives them excuses not to do anything. Definition of potential: Ain't done sh!t yet!**"**

Final Thoughts

This is an excellent time to go **hmmm** and ask yourself what you've learned and what you can immediately apply to achieve better results in your life.

Many times throughout my career, I've been asked for recommendations for good books to read. And while there are certainly a plethora of books to choose from, my comment has always been: "It's not a matter of how many books you read, it's more about mastering the books you read." You see, if all someone does is read book after book after book, they have only gained the capacity of being smarter. But without the clear comprehension of what they've read and without mastering and applying the context of what they've read, they are, unfortunately, not any better. **Hmmm.** Consider the millions of people who've read the classic "self-help" and "wealth-help" book *Think and Grow Rich* by Napoleon Hill. What percentage of those individuals do you think have gone on to be "rich" in whatever endeavor they chose? Wouldn't you say a small percentage? Why is that? Do you think it's because the book's philosophies don't really work? Of course not. It's because reading a book like that once won't allow you to comprehend it and apply it. You have to read it until you master it!

You decided to read my book so the same principle holds true here. Read it once and you say **hmmm** and maybe you're a little smarter. Read it again and again and you will not only say **hmmm** but also you will probably be a lot smarter, and even more importantly, you will also be on your way to getting a lot better because you're now applying what you've read. Always remember, being better is always more beneficial and rewarding than being smarter. One final **hmmm,** I couldn't help myself. So, read, read, and read again and begin to apply these **hmmms** to your everyday life, both personally and professionally, and experience the best of success, prosperity, and, most importantly, fulfillment in every area of your life.

Stay tuned for more impactful
Hmmms
in the future!